GETTING TO KNOW JESUS

WHAT DO MATTHEW, MARK, LUKE, AND JOHN TELL US?

JUAN ALFARO

Liguori

ONE LIGUORI DRIVE
LIGUORI MO 63057-9999

Imprimi Potest:
Thomas D. Picton, C.Ss.R.
Provincial, Denver Province
The Redemptorists

Published by Liguori
Liguori, Missouri
www.liguori.org

ISBN 978-0-7648-1727-4

Liguori Publications, a nonprofit corporation, is an apostolate of the Redemptorists. To learn more about the Redemptorists, visit *Redemptorists.com.*

Printed in the United States of America
11 10 09 08   4 2 3 1
First edition

*I dedicate this work to two professors of holy Scripture with whom
I had a special relationship: Father Ignace de la Potterie, S.J.,
Professor of the Pontifical Biblical Institute of Rome, who helped me
in my studies on the Gospel of Saint John, and
Father John Linskens, C.I.C.M., with whom I worked for years,
listening to his prophetic vision of the Gospel of Saint Luke.*

CONTENTS

INTRODUCTION

Many readers of some of my biblical works written in Spanish have asked me to publish some of them in English so that bilingual communities can benefit more. At their request I have written this book in both languages to introduce the Gospels so that readers can know and love Jesus more deeply, and get to know better the message of each Gospel.

To know Jesus is to know the Gospels, and the knowledge of the Gospels should lead to knowledge of Jesus. But knowing Jesus is not just a function of the brain; it is, above all, a challenge to the heart. The knowledge of Jesus must be immersed in the love of Jesus, so that we can live with him and for him, so that we can incarnate him in our own life and behavior. Einstein said that a person cannot read the Gospel without feeling the presence of Jesus. His person is reflected in every one of his words. Jesus in the Gospel is life, and this life is experienced and known when we live his Word.

Only those who love Jesus intensely come to know him well. Many people have lived their life believing they loved Jesus to discover one day, like Saint Augustine, that very late they have come to reach the depth of love Jesus desires from us. We start to know Jesus when we are children with our minds; finally, we come to truly know him with our hearts.

This book has been arranged to begin with the general themes related to the Gospels and their composition, with some points of interest related to the apocryphal gospels. Then the fundamentals of each of the Gospels are presented with their basic teachings to cover gradually the most important texts, looking more to feed the faith and the spiritual needs of the readers than to satisfy their curiosity.

1
GENERAL THEMES

1. Why are the books on the life of Jesus called "Gospels"?

Saint Mark called his book a "gospel," a Greek word that literally means "good news" (Mk 1:1). This term is already used in the Old Testament (see Isaiah 52:7 and 61:1) in reference to the end of the Babylonian captivity and the joyful announcement of the liberation of the people of Israel.

Saint Mark says that Jesus preached the Gospel (Good News) (Mk 1:15), asking for a response of faith and repentance. Saint Luke, also quoting the prophet Isaiah, presents Jesus announcing the Good News to the poor (see Lk 4:16–21). This Good News must be received with faith and joy, with a spirit of docility and obedience.

A great piece of news becomes either good or bad news when it affects the life of the receiver. The news that someone won a big prize in a lottery in Nebraska has little meaning for someone in Texas or California, but if the news is that the winner is someone from your city or your street, or one of your relatives, it becomes very good news for you, because in some way you will share the benefits of that news.

If the Gospel is to become truly good news for a person, it has to be received and accepted with faith so that the message of Jesus goes into the recipient's heart and affects that person's life. The Gospel calls the person to conversion—giving light, consolation, and hope—with joy to face the problems and challenges of daily life. The Gospel should not be read merely to learn about Jesus, but to enrich our relationship with Jesus himself and to direct our life toward other persons, in love.

2. Is the Gospel's Good News just for the poor, or is it also for the rich?

Saint Luke quotes the prophet Isaiah, saying that the Gospel is Good News for the poor (see Is 61:1; Lk 4:18), for those who are in need of God, for those who are hungry and thirsty for justice, for the humble, the sick, and the handicapped. Wealth and poverty are material realities that affect the lives of every person and especially affect our hearts and dispositions. For Saint Luke, poverty created and imposed on people is a sin, a fruit of sin, and should be eradicated; whereas poverty accepted voluntarily, as a means to help others, is a virtue that liberates people from attachment to material things and disposes them to help liberate the poor from their material poverty. Voluntary poverty enables a person to find greater personal freedom through renunciation.

There certainly are rich persons who know how to be generous and share with the needy. These individuals are, in a way, poor in spirit. There are other people who are materially poor but are dying from a desire to become rich, and their behavior is selfish and closed to others. Nevertheless, it is important to note that it is easier to be generous and open to God and to others for people who have fewer material goods; those with many possessions can easily become slaves to their wealth. This happened to the rich young man in the Gospel who could not renounce his wealth to follow Jesus (see Mk 10:17–22).

Jesus pointed out that it would be a miracle if the rich enter the kingdom of heaven—"It is easier for a camel to go through the eye of a needle"—because of their attachment to their possessions (Mk 10:25). It would also take a miracle for the rich to receive and appreciate truly the Gospel, the book of the kingdom, by listening to the invitation to conversion; the rich generally seek to justify themselves, to affirm their way of life, without changing and answering the call to conversion. The rich, sometimes without being aware of it, try to make the Gospel "good news for the rich." Only when the rich accept the Gospel in their heart and are moved to share their wealth with the needy will they truly become poor in spirit, and the Gospel will be good news for them as well. The conversion of Zacchaeus, the wealthy tax collector who gave half of his goods to the poor, will always be a good model for the rich of every period (see Lk 19:1–10).

3. What is the *oral gospel*?

The *oral gospel* is a term used for the period after the resurrection of Jesus during which apostles, disciples, and deacons preached the message of Jesus. In The Acts of the Apostles we can see that the message was centered on the mystery of Christ: the passion, death, resurrection, ascension, and the gift of the Spirit. Later, more details were added on the life of Jesus and his ministry, designed to build up the faith of believers and to provide direction on how to live the novelty of the Christian message.

The message and the narrations about Jesus were passed along by word of mouth among the members of the Christian communities. For forty years the Gospel was announced orally. It is possible that during this period some of the sayings and actions of Jesus began to be put in writing. The stories about Jesus were repeated and enriched with details that could be more significant for the faith and the life of the community or group to which they were directed.

Stories that are repeated frequently tend to take a fixed form of expression. Miracles could be narrated stressing the length and seriousness of the sickness; a healing might be accompanied by a profession of faith and usually would happen right away; the admiration of the crowd would close the narration. An important saying of Jesus could be placed in the context of a short incident as the end and climax of the narration (see Mk 2:15–17, 18–22, 23–28). These forms of narration started with the oral preaching of the Gospel and are often found in the written Gospels.

The writers of the four Gospels, inspired by the Holy Spirit, had to choose among the many stories circulating about Jesus ("…the world itself could not contain the books that would be written"; Jn 21:25)—those they considered more effective to lead their future readers to faith in Jesus. The writers also had to determine the order in which it was effective to place the narrations, although it was clear that the ministry of Jesus began with his baptism in the Jordan River and ended in Jerusalem with the passion and resurrection. Other stories and sayings of Jesus were placed in the order each evangelist chose to build up the faith of his readers.

4. Why do we have only four Gospels?

Since the earliest times the Catholic Church has recognized as inspired only the four Gospels we have in the Bible now: Matthew, Mark, Luke, and John. In the second century, the first apocryphal gospels started to appear; they were generally prepared by heretics who wanted to justify their points of view with the help of presumed religious texts. The Catholic Church has never accepted such gospels as inspired.

Among the oldest texts that speak about the books inspired by God is the Muratorian Fragment, a text from the second century that reads:

> The third Gospel, the book according to Luke. This Luke, a physician, after the ascension of Christ, was taken as a traveling companion by Paul. He wrote according to his investigations, although he had not known personally the Lord....
>
> John, the fourth of the gospels, wrote at the request of his disciples and the desire of the other apostles and bishops, telling them: Let us fast for three days, and then let us narrate to each other whatever is revealed to us. That same night, it was revealed to the apostle Andrew that John should be the one to write.... (*Enchiridium Biblicum*, Roma, 1961).

The well-known Catechetic Lectures, written by Saint Cyril of Jerusalem, bishop of that city, in the fourth century, teach:

> In the New Testament there are four gospels. The others are false and harmful. Manichean heretics wrote a gospel according to Thomas, which with the false title of gospel leads souls and simple people astray.

Many other documents from the fourth century, after persecutions of the Church stopped, mention the four Gospels without naming them, because they are supposed to be known and accepted by all.

5. Is it providential that we have four Gospels instead of just one?

The four Gospels were written for Christian communities very different from each other. This was providential since great differences among the believers from various times and places have always existed.

Saint Matthew wrote his Gospel for Christians converted from Judaism; thus he stresses that Christians are the New Israel of God in whom the promises and prophecies of the Old Testament are being fulfilled. Saint Matthew insists on obedience to the teachings of Jesus; he seems to face the fact that the new believers have their roots in a people who had become notorious for disobedience and a stiff neck (see Ex 32:9; 33:5; 34:9; Dt 1:26–27, 41–46; 9:7–14; Acts 7:51–53).

Saint Mark wrote for Christians who had suffered persecution under the Roman emperor Nero, the most powerful man in the world of that time. Saint Mark seeks to encourage Christians, a humble and powerless group, presenting Jesus to them as the almighty; with Jesus on their side, Christians should not fear anything or anybody.

Saint Luke wrote for Christians who lived in the midst of a Greco-Roman world, where great social inequities were the rule. Saint Luke insists on the duties of Christians toward the poor and the needy.

Saint John seems to write for a somewhat charismatic group that lived in tension within a Jewish and Greek world. He wants to strengthen their faith by proposing a Christian ideal of imitation and identification with Jesus, who will bring them to a perfect joy.

We are fortunate to have four Gospels with such different characteristics. Sometimes we might feel rebellious and disobedient toward the Lord or toward the Church; then we shall benefit from reading the Gospel of Matthew. Persons who feel depressed and powerless are inspired by the Gospel of Mark. The Gospel of Luke is always a good reminder to the rich of their social responsibilities toward the poor. Persons filled with devotion and a desire to be more like Jesus benefit from reading the Gospel of John. It is providential that we have four Gospels instead of just one.

6. What are the apocryphal gospels?

The word *apocryphal* means occult, but in Spanish the word refers to something *fabulous* or *faked,* something that lacks authenticity with regard to the contents or to the author of the material. The apocryphal gospels are a series of writings about the life of Jesus that started to appear in the second century.

For the Catholic Church, the apocryphal gospels are false not just because most of their contents are not true, but principally because the authors pretended to be inspired by God when in reality they were not. Some of the early Church Fathers quote texts from these apocryphal gospels because they considered that some of their contents about Jesus and his teachings might be authentic.

Many apocryphal gospels deal with the *infancy* and with the *passion* of Jesus. The authors seek to satisfy the curiosity and devotion of some of the faithful. They invented fantastic happenings and extravagant legends about details of the life of Jesus that are not found in the four canonical Gospels. In these gospels one can detect the beginnings of an incipient Christian theology about Jesus and Mary.

A good division of the apocryphal gospels is one rooted on their origins and characteristics:

- *Judeo-Christian gospels* that reflect the tensions of the early Church of the second century, dealing with its Jewish roots and observances. Such are the *Gospel of the Hebrews, the Gospel of the Nazarenes, the Gospel of the Ebionites,* and so on.
- *There are gospels attributed to persons associated with Jesus* in the canonical Gospels; they contain fantastic (and sometimes repugnant) legends and miracles about the infancy of Jesus and the life of Mary. Most of them originated in the third and fourth centuries: *Gospels of Peter, James, Nicodemus, Bartholomew,* and so on.
- *Gnostic gospels* often claim to contain secret teachings of Jesus not found in our four Gospels. The contents are attributed to some persons closely associated with Jesus, such as *Saint John, Saint Thomas,* and even *to Judas the traitor.*

7. Lately there has been talk about the gospels of Thomas and Judas. Is it true that the Catholic Church tried to hide and suppress them?

A gospel attributed to Saint Thomas has been the object of much talk in recent times (there was already another apocryphal gospel attributed to Thomas); it was found in Egypt in a place called Nag Hammadi. This gospel, as was done with another attributed to Judas, has been presented by publicity seekers, in the press, and on television as a gospel that the Church attempted to suppress.

This gospel of Thomas contains a collection of 114 sayings or pronouncements attributed to Jesus and revealed to Saint Thomas. Some of the sayings are similar to some in the canonical Gospels; others are openly heretical and of Gnostic origin. The teachings are presented as revealed by the glorious Jesus after his resurrection. The Catholic Church realized very soon that this gospel could not be considered inspired by God.

At first, some commentators thought that it was a primitive gospel, contemporary with the four canonical Gospels, akin to the discourses of Jesus found in the Gospels of Matthew and Luke. At present, experts believe that this gospel was written in the second century to support heretical doctrines of Gnosticism that pretended to know secret roads to salvation reserved to those initiated in the secrets of their sects.

The these samples from the gospel of Thomas speak for themselves:

- Jesus said: I have thrown fire into the world; I keep it until it burns (10).
- A man is like an intelligent fisherman who cast his net and brought it out filled with small fish. When among them he found a big and good one, the intelligent fisherman threw the small ones into the sea and chose the big one without delay (8).
- Jesus said: He who is near me is near the fire; he who is far from me is far from the Kingdom (82).
- The disciples said to Jesus: We know that you will go away from us. Who will be the greatest among us? Jesus answered: wherever you gather together, go to James the Just through whom heaven and earth were made (12).
- Jesus said: The Kingdom of Heaven is like a man who wanted to kill a giant. He took the sword in his house and struck the wall to test the strength of his arm. Later he killed the giant (98).
- Jesus said: Woe to the Pharisees: they are like a dog resting on the manger of the oxen; they neither eat nor let the oxen eat. (Aurelio de Santos Otero, *Los Evangelios apócricos,* BAC, Madrid, 2002).

8. What are some of the principal teachings of the apocryphal gospels?

Although the apocryphal gospels contain generally false information, many contain details that have become part of popular piety and are found in Christian art. Some of the stories of the apocryphal gospels serve to explain the beliefs of early Christians; they also deal with themes that the canonical Gospels left open.

The gospels of the Infancy of Jesus offer data on his family that cannot be corroborated from other sources, such as the names of the parents of Mary (Joachim and Anne); the miraculous birth of Mary; the presentation on Mary in the Temple at age three; how Saint Joseph was chosen to be the guardian of Mary and Jesus, and so on. The gospels of the infancy multiply miracles around the birth of Jesus and the miracles Jesus performed as a young boy. These narrations want to affirm that Jesus was the Incarnated God, all-powerful, from the beginning of his life on earth.

There are also narrations that affirmed some beliefs of the early Church that are still valid now, such as the holiness and the perpetual virginity of Mary. We read in them of the "dormition" or sleep of Mary, suggesting her assumption into heaven. The perfect association of Mary with her Son Jesus has been stated since the early days of the Church. The stories of the apocryphal gospels were invented to explain, or give a reason, for that early faith that predated those gospels.

9. What is the meaning of the word *synoptic* when it is applied to the Gospels?

The first three Gospels are called *synoptic* because they are so similar in their structure, contents, and even vocabulary that a person, having seen or read one of them, in some way has also already seen or read the others. It could be said that the first Gospels are twins or triplets.

When a family has three identical children, only people close to that family are able to distinguish them; others are confused by their similar resemblances. If the mother of the children is asked how she distinguishes them since they are so identical, she might answer stressing their differences in their mannerisms, reactions, the tone of their voices, their way of doing things, their preferences, dreams, whims, temperament, and interests. Something similar happens with the first three Gospels. Those who know them well can better appreciate how much they differ from each other.

Although the first three Gospels are very similar and they sometimes use the same words in some narrations, many details in the stories show how much they differ. Each evangelist had in mind the particular community for which he was writing and had his own goals and personal preferences. People who are not very familiar with the Gospels tend to mix the narrations of one with that of the other, sometimes falsifying the message that the evangelist wanted to transmit. Often this is seen in television evangelists who mix up biblical texts, often taking them out of context, to make them say what the preacher wants and not what the original writer intended. The Catholic Church has always made an effort to be faithful to the message that the inspired authors, and God through them, wanted to transmit to us.

10. What are the reasons for the similarities and differences found in the synoptic Gospels?

This question corresponds to what is known as the *synoptic problem*. Over the past two centuries several theories or solutions have been proposed to explain this phenomenon so clear and so unique in world literature.

The three synoptic Gospels present the activity of Jesus along the same general lines: preparation with the ministry of John the Baptist, the ministry of Jesus in Galilee, the trip to Jerusalem, the ministry in Jerusalem, the passion, and the resurrection.

The most acceptable theory regarding the written composition of the Gospels (not considering that the Gospel was preached and adapted orally for half a century after the death of Jesus) proposes that originally there were two written documents on the life of Jesus, the theory of the *two sources;* one was the Gospel of Mark, and the other a collection of sermons and sayings of the Lord. Saints Matthew and Luke would have copied part of their Gospels from these two primitive sources; they also added personal information that they obtained from other sources whose origin we do not currently know.

It is clear that when two narrations coincide verbatim in their details, it must be due to the fact that an author copied from the other or that both of them copied from a common source. There are some narrations found in the first three Gospels (Matthew, Mark, and Luke); these constitute the *triple tradition* that has at its base the Gospel of Mark. Some narrations are found only in Matthew and Luke; they constitute the *double tradition,* which includes principally discourses and sayings of Jesus. Authors suppose that both evangelists copied from a document called Q *(Quelle,* in German *source).* Many of the differences in the details of the narrations can be explained from the oral tradition that every evangelist knew and adapted to the interests of his readers and to his personal aims and preferences.

11. Which of the Gospels is the most important?

As noted previously, it is providential that we have four Gospels instead of just one, since they correspond to the needs of the communities for which they were written and they can very well correspond to the different needs and situations of our world today. The importance of a thing or a text sometimes depends on a person's particular conditions or situations; it is something relatively subjective.

Objectively, all four Gospels are equally important, since they transmit to us a message from God about Jesus our Savior. Persons seeking spiritual food for their hearts will surely find it in each of the Gospels they read. Persons seeking a medicine or remedy for their personal problems or difficulties in the Gospels must accompany their reading with prayer and meditation so that they can better listen to the message of the Lord.

I will never tire of repeating what I said in answering question #5: "We are fortunate to have four Gospels with such different characteristics. Sometimes we might feel rebellious and disobedient toward the Lord or toward the Church; then we shall benefit from reading the Gospel of Matthew. Persons who feel depressed and powerless are inspired by the Gospel of Mark. The Gospel of Luke is always a good reminder to the rich of their social responsibilities toward the poor. Persons filled with devotion and a desire to be more like Jesus benefit from reading the Gospel of John. It is providential that we have four Gospels instead of just one."

12. When were the Gospels written?

The four Gospels were written after a long process of oral preaching for several decades after the resurrection and ascension of Jesus. The original preaching centered on the passion and resurrection of the Lord. Later, other teachings of Jesus were gradually added in additions to many incidents of his ministry as a means to feed and strengthen the faith and commitment of believers.

A very old tradition states that the first to write a Gospel was Saint Matthew, who wrote it in the Aramaic language. Nothing has been found about his Gospel, although in the four Gospels we find traditions that seem to have been transmitted first in the Aramaic language and later expressed in Greek. Saint Luke says that by the time he wrote his Gospel, others had written already about the ministry of Jesus; we do not know to which writings Saint Luke was referring.

Generally it is believed that the first of our current four Gospels was written by Saint Mark, since Saint Matthew and Saint Luke depend on Saint Mark's text. Saint Mark could have written his Gospel at the end of the reign of Roman emperor Nero, after the death of the apostles Peter and Paul, between the years AD 65 and 70. Saint Mark seems to have in mind a community that has suffered persecution; he invites Christians to look to Jesus for inspiration and strength.

The Gospel of Saint Matthew seems to reflect the conflicts of the early Church with Jewish authorities of Palestine, after the destruction of Jerusalem by the Romans. It was probably written about AD 80.

Saint Luke, a companion of Saint Paul in some of his travels, was an educated person who wrote his Gospel to present the message of Jesus for Christian communities that increasingly included members converted from paganism who resided in the midst of the Roman and Greek worlds. It is probable that he wrote around the time of AD 85 to 90.

The Gospel of Saint John, which many considered to be written last, now is considered by some as an early Gospel, not too distant from the Gospel of Mark, with whom he has good correlation. It is probable that the author of the fourth Gospel wrote his work about AD 70 and later revised it and added new materials about AD 90. These dates raise the question of whether this Gospel had just one author with two different editions of his work.

13. Who were the real authors of the Gospels?

Two of the Gospels are attributed to apostles who lived with Jesus: Matthew and John. The other two are attributed to disciples of the apostles or to persons who lived in contact with them.

Some biblical experts think the apostles were persons with little literary education, almost illiterate, incapable themselves of writing the works attributed to them. However, we should remember that in antiquity the word *author* did not have the meaning it has at present. A person could be considered an author when the work was written by someone else, under his direction or inspiration, without personally writing it.

The authors of the Gospels of Matthew and John could have been disciples of these apostles, who gathered their teachings and so attributed the work to the persons who had inspired them. Some think that these Gospels could have been the result of a collective work, a kind of school that wanted to transmit the doctrine of their teacher.

The Gospel of Saint Mark, like that of Saint Luke, was probably written by a single author, exclusively responsible for his work. Luke's Gospel, with the second part of his work, The Acts of the Apostles, reveals a person highly educated with literary knowledge not common in his time.

14. What does the Second Vatican Council teach about the Gospels?

The bishops of the entire world, gathered in Rome for the Second Vatican Council, approved the Dogmatic Constitution on Divine Revelation *(Dei Verbum)* on November 18, 1965. I had the privilege of being present at that memorable session of the Council together with many students from the Pontifical Biblical Institute of Rome.

The bishops made a magnificent synthesis of the Church's teachings on the Sacred Scripture and its meaning for our time. The fifth chapter of the *Constitution,* named in Latin *Dei Verbum* or *Word of God,* contains the teaching on the New Testament, with special references to the Gospels. Some of the most basic points that are important to remember are the following:

> **No. 17:** The word of God, which is the power of God for the salvation of all who believe (see Romans 1:16), is set forth and shows its power in a most excellent way in the writings of the New Testament.

> **No. 18:** It is common knowledge that among all the Scriptures, even those of the New Testament, the Gospels have a special preeminence, and rightly so, for they are the principal witness for the life and teaching of the incarnate Word, our savior.

> The Church has always and everywhere held and continues to hold that the four Gospels are of apostolic origin. For what the Apostles preached in fulfillment of the commission of Christ, afterwards they themselves and apostolic men, under the inspiration of the divine Spirit, handed on to us in writing: the foundation of faith, namely, the fourfold Gospel, according to Matthew, Mark, Luke and John.

> **No. 19:** Holy Mother Church has firmly and with absolute constancy held, and continues to hold, that the four Gospels

just named, whose historical character the Church unhesitatingly asserts, faithfully hand on what Jesus Christ, while living among men, really did and taught for their eternal salvation until the day He was taken up into heaven (see Acts 1:1). Indeed, after the Ascension of the Lord the Apostles handed on to their hearers what He had said and done. This they did with that clearer understanding which they enjoyed after they had been instructed by the glorious events of Christ's life and taught by the light of the Spirit of truth. The sacred authors wrote the four Gospels, selecting some things from the many which had been handed on by word of mouth or in writing, reducing some of them to a synthesis, explaining some things in view of the situation of their churches and preserving the form of proclamation but always in such fashion that they told us the honest truth about Jesus. For their intention in writing was that either from their own memory and recollections, or from the witness of those who "themselves from the beginning were eyewitnesses and ministers of the Word" we might know "the truth" concerning those matters about which we have been instructed (see Luke 1:2–4).

15. What does the Catholic Church teach regarding fundamentalism and the correct interpretation of the Gospels?

Fundamentalism originated during the Protestant Reformation from a desire to be faithful to the literal meaning of the Scriptures. For the past two hundred years, fundamentalism has been mostly a reaction against liberal and rationalist exegesis from Germany and France. The word *fundamentalism* is associated directly with an American Biblical Congress celebrated at Niagara, New York, in 1895. Protestant conservative interpreters determined what they considered to be five fundamental tenets of the Christian faith: (1) the verbal and unerring inspiration of the Bible, (2) the virgin birth of Jesus, (3) the doctrine of the vicarious expiation of our sins by Jesus, (4) the corporal resurrection of Christians, and (5) the Second Coming of Jesus. Over the past 150 years, fundamentalism has spread and strengthened in the United States.

One of the most important documents of the Catholic Church on the interpretation of the holy Scriptures was prepared by the Pontifical

Biblical Commission and promulgated by Pope John Paul II on April 23, 1993. It is titled "The Interpretation of the Bible in the Church." This document contains an important section on fundamentalism. Some of the teaching points on this important topic, stressing the principal ideas, are quoted below:

> Fundamentalism often shows a tendency to ignore or to deny the problems presented by the biblical text in its original Hebrew, Aramaic or Greek form. It is often narrowly bound to one fixed translation, whether old or present-day. By the same token it fails to take account of the "rereadings" of certain texts which are found within the Bible itself.
>
> In what concerns the Gospels, fundamentalism does not take into account the development of the Gospel tradition, but naively confuses the final stage of this tradition (what the evangelists have written) with the initial (the words and deeds of the historical Jesus). At the same time fundamentalism neglects an important fact: The way in which the first Christian communities themselves understood the impact produced by Jesus of Nazareth and his message. But it is precisely there that we find a witness to the apostolic origin of the Christian faith and its direct expressions. Fundamentalism thus misrepresents the call voiced by the Gospel itself.
>
> Fundamentalism likewise tends to adopt very narrow points of view. It accepts the literal reality of an ancient, out-of-date cosmology simply because it is found expressed in the Bible; this blocks any dialogue with a broader way of seeing the relationship between culture and faith. Its relying upon a non-critical reading of certain texts of the bible serves to re-inforce political ideas and social attitudes that are marked by prejudices—racism, for example—quite contrary to the Christian Gospel.
>
> Finally, in its attachment to the principle "Scripture alone," fundamentalism separates the interpretation of the Bible from the tradition, which, guided by the Spirit, has authentically developed in union with Scripture in the heart of the community of faith. It fails to realize that the New Testament took form

within the Christian church and that it is the Holy Scripture of this church, the existence of which preceded the composition of the texts. Because of this, fundamentalism is often anti-church, it considers of little importance the creeds, the doctrines, and liturgical practices that have become part of church tradition, as well as the teaching function of the church itself. It presents itself as a form of private interpretation that does not acknowledge that the church is founded on the Bible and draws its life and inspiration from Scripture.

The fundamentalist approach is dangerous, for it is attractive to people who look to the Bible for ready answers to the problems of life. It can deceive these people, offering them interpretations that are pious but illusory, instead of telling them that the Bible does not necessarily contain an immediate answer to each and every problem. Without saying as much in so many words, fundamentalism actually invites people to a kind of intellectual suicide. It injects into life a false certitude, for it unwittingly confuses the divine substance of the biblical message with what are in fact its human limitations.

2

THE GOSPEL
OF SAINT MATTHEW

16. What was the goal of Saint Matthew
in writing his Gospel?

During the first decades after the ascension, Jews who converted to Christianity in Palestine were considered religiously as a branch of Judaism. The apostles continued going to the Jerusalem Temple for prayers and vows. Christians were considered one of the new branches of Judaism, as were the Pharisees, Sadducees, and Essenees (see Acts 2:46; 3:1; 5:12, 20–21; 21:26; 23:6).

The final break of Christians with Jews was possibly linked to the destruction of Jerusalem by the Romans in AD 70. When the entire Jewish nation fought for freedom and independence from the Romans, Palestinian Christians, according to an old tradition, probably did not participate in the struggle and moved to the city of Pella on the other side of the Jordan River. After the destruction of Jerusalem, Christians were possibly seen as traitors to the country and religion because they had not participated in the defense of the homeland. The break was total.

The destruction of Jerusalem and its Temple, combined with the loss of the land, created a crisis in the hopes and expectations of Jews. They questioned how God could have permitted such an event and wondered about the future of Judaism and the promises of God to the Israel of old. Toward the year AD 90 there were three answers or opinions regarding this question:

1. Jewish rabbis, mostly from the group of the Pharisees, believed that the future of Israel was in the hands of God and depended on the fidelity of Jews to the Law of Moses. Without a land and a Temple,

the Bible was going to become their point of salvation and means of communion with God.

2. Authors of apocalyptic books believed that the present world was about to end and give way to a future world through a direct intervention of God and of his Messiah. They were not to worry too much about the existing condition since it was about to end; they just needed faith and patience, with a faithful observance of the prescriptions of the Law of Moses.

3. In his Gospel, Saint Matthew offered a new response to the questions of the present and to the hopes for the future. Christians are the heirs of the promises of the Old Testament, the New Israel of God. The long-awaited "new world" expected for the end time had arrived with the passion and resurrection of Jesus; the Jews had expected a resurrection at the end of the world. Saint Matthew announces that the end of the world has come with Jesus, and many holy people who had died were resurrected with Jesus (see Mt 27:52–53). The Israel of the promises is now found in the Christian community for which Saint Matthew writes his Gospel.

The New Israel has been born with Jesus who is the *God-with-us* (see Mt 1:23) who is going to be forever with his people (see Mt 28:20), just as God had been with the people of the Old Israel. The New Israel, like the old, is born in the midst of a sacrifice of innocent children and finds refuge precisely in Egypt—the place where the Old Israel had begun. The promises of God find their fulfillment and meaning in the New Israel. The Christian community will live again, at a deeper level, the values and traditions of the Old Israel, through a presence and assistance from God revealed in Jesus.

17. What is the general structure and content of Matthew's Gospel?

The Gospel of Saint Matthew, written for Christians converted from Judaism, has clear perspectives and teachings derived from the Old Testament, but some readers see in it some of the harshest condemnations of the Jews of that time. If this is partially true, it might be because Matthew wanted to convince his readers that they were the authentic heirs of the promises made to ancient Israel.

Matthew attacks the scribes and Pharisees, the religious leaders of the people of Israel after the destruction of Jerusalem, who were bitterly opposed to the new Christian faith. Some have seen in this Gospel the roots of the anti-Semitism of some Christians through the centuries in the famous statement of the Jews reported during the passion of Jesus: "His blood be on us and on our children!" (Mt 27:25).

Saint Matthew divided his Gospel into three sections: the infancy of Jesus, the ministry in Galilee, and the ministry in Jerusalem with the passion and resurrection. The ministry of Jesus is presented along five great sermons, which conclude with the same formula and which may have in mind the five books of the law of Moses. The sermons are:

1. The Sermon on the Mount (Mt 5—7)
2. The Missionary Sermon (Mt 10)
3. The Sermon of Parables (Mt 13)
4. The Ecclesiastical Sermon (Mt 18)
5. The Eschatological Sermon (Mt 24—25)

Interspersed among these five sermons are narrative sections that prepare the theme of the sermon that follows. These sermons present the kingdom of God from its initial preaching to its consummation. The Christian community is the New Israel, which rises above all the hopes and practices of the old.

18. What is the principal image of Jesus that Saint Matthew offers readers of his Gospel?

The first and the last images of Jesus offered by Matthew are those of Jesus as God, the Son of the Father, born of a virgin, the *God-with-us* or Emmanuel (Mt 1:23) and the Jesus who is God and has all power in heaven and on earth and who is going to be with his disciples until the end of the world (Mt 28:18–20). Jesus speaks as God and makes the same kind of promise that God made in the Old Testament, promising his help, when he sent leaders and prophets for missions in which human strength seemed insufficient for the task (see Ex 3:12; Dt 31:8, 23; Jos 1:5, 9; Jer 1:8).

Jesus is also the incarnation of a New Israel, the Christian community that is born in him and with him, and suffers persecution and adversities like the Old Israel. Jesus is also the promised Messiah, the

Son of David, the one the Jews had been waiting for, but very different from what they had expected; he did not come to affirm the prejudices, weaknesses, and false hopes of the Jews of his time but to call them to conversion and renewal.

Jesus is the Son of the Father, revealing to us that his Father is our Father, too. Jesus is the servant of the Lord (see Mt 12:18–11), who fulfills the mission entrusted to him by the Father. He is also, like God in the Old Testament, the shepherd who is going to take care of the flock of the Lord (see Mt 9:36; 10:6; 12:9–14). He is the ideal Teacher and Guide who directs his disciples teaching them the way to life (see Mt 23:8–12).

19. Why is Saint Matthew's work called the *ecclesial Gospel?*

The Gospel of Matthew has been called the *ecclesial Gospel* since it calls the Christian community *the Church* (see Mt 18:17). Also, the Gospel of Matthew is the one that has been most used in the liturgy of the Catholic Church throughout the centuries. Until the reform of the liturgical Lectionary, after the Second Vatican Council, for about thirty-five Sundays we read Matthew's Gospel at Mass. The Gospel of John was read in some Sundays of Lent and Easter. Because of this fact, Catholics were accustomed to thinking of and expressing their faith most often in terms of the teachings of the Gospel of Matthew.

For Saint Matthew, the Christian community is the assembly of those called and gathered by God, with all members as sons and daughters of the same Father, with absolute equality among them; they are not to take on titles, to put themselves above others. There can be faults and sins among the members, so all will be called to forgive one another and to exercise fraternal correction.

20. Which is the most important virtue for a Christian according to Saint Matthew?

While writing his Gospel, Saint Matthew had in mind Christians converted from Judaism; maybe because of this, he had in mind the most common sin of Old Israel that he does not want to see repeated in the Church—the disobedience of the "stiff-necked people" was a common sin of Israel in the Old Testament. For Saint Matthew, Christians must distinguish themselves for their obedience and fidelity to the words of Jesus.

The obedience and fidelity of the Christian must show itself in actions, not just in words: "Not everyone who says to me, 'Lord, Lord,' will enter the kingdom of heaven, but only the one who does the will of my Father in heaven" (Mt 7:21). This idea of fidelity and obedience to the teachings of Jesus is stressed at the end of the Sermon on the Mount: "And everyone who hears these words of mine and does not act on them will be like a foolish man who built his house on sand. The rain fell, and the floods came, and the winds blew and beat against that house, and it fell—and great was its fall!" (Mt 7:26–27).

Obedience to the words of Jesus must show itself in actions, so that a good person is not one who does no wrong but one who does good to others, especially to the poor and the needy. This idea is underlined in the narration of the Final Judgment where those condemned are those who did nothing when there was a duty or an opportunity to do good (see Mt 25:31–46). Naturally, those who stole the food and clothing, those who closed their doors to the poor and put them in jails will go to hell by themselves, without waiting for God to pass a sentence on them.

21. Where did Matthew obtain the stories about the infancy of Jesus (Mt 1—2)?

The stories of the infancy of Jesus in Matthew have no parallels in the other Gospels. It is supposed that he obtained them from sources we know nothing about. Some, however, believe that Saint Matthew wrote them by himself, inspired himself by texts from the Old Testament.

So, while many interpreters see in these narrations events that actually happened, there are others who think that Saint Matthew, in this section of the infancy, used the narrative style called *midrash* in Hebrew, that is, a manner of developing stories that constitute a kind of theological reflection on the origins of Jesus, using texts from the Old Testament, giving them new life and meaning.

Saint Matthew seems to operate in the stories of the infancy of Jesus at a double level: while telling us the origin and the mission of Jesus, he is also telling us the origin and mission of the Christian community, which for the evangelist is the New Israel of God, which in many ways recalls the birth of the Old Israel.

The contents of the stories of the infancy, especially those related to the behavior of King Herod, are very much in agreement with what is known about this king from sources outside the Bible.

22. What is the function or mission of Joseph in Matthew's Gospel (Mt 1:18–25)?

Saint Matthew narrates the infancy of Jesus from the perspective of Saint Joseph, while Saint Luke narrates it from the perspective of Mary. Although Joseph is not the father of Jesus (who is born from a virgin), Joseph receives the mission of acting as father of the child: He will give the name to the child and, most importantly, will pass on to Jesus the messianic title of *Son of David* see (Mt 1:20), a title that will be given to Jesus in special moments of his public life (see Mt 20:30–31; 21:9; 22:41–46).

The narration of the annunciation to Joseph seems to imply that Saint Joseph knew the mystery of the conception of Jesus from the lips of Mary; Joseph believed her, even if it seemed something unbelievable. Joseph had faith in Mary. When Joseph realized that God had taken a hand in the life of Mary, Joseph decided to step aside. The angel told him, "Do not be afraid"—a biblical phrase that marks a human response in the presence of a divine action or apparition. If Joseph believed that God had acted in Mary, he was ready to step aside so as not to interfere with God's plans. But Joseph was to be part of the divine plan for the life of Jesus. The message of the angel "in a dream" is the device chosen by Matthew to indicate a divine communication; he repeats it in the infancy narrative (see Mt 1:20; 2:12, 19, 22).

The narration about Saint Joseph concludes with a quote from Scripture in which Catholics, and many Protestants, see the virgin birth of Jesus, and even the perpetual virginity of Mary. The quote culminates in the last phrase that becomes the climax of the announcement: The child to be born is a *God-with-us,* a new presence of God in the history of his people, the New Israel.

23. The story of the Magi (Mt 2:1–12)—is it true or is it a legend?

This question supposes that there is some question regarding truth and legend, but we must remember that in antiquity many legends were used as a means to teach great truths. Rather than asking what happened or how something happened, one should consider the purpose of the author's writing and what he wanted to teach through his narration.

Saint Matthew, like Saint Luke, places the birth of Jesus in Bethlehem, the birthplace of King David, a place where messianic Jewish hopes were centered. If Jesus was born during the reign of King Herod, the date of Jesus' birth should be moved about seven years before our present Christian era, for we now know that our calendar is in error.

The Magi could be persons belonging to a group of astronomers or astrologers from Persia or Babylon, who saw a star or a convergence of planets that they considered an omen for the birth of an important person. Astronomers tell us today that there was such a convergence of planets about the year 7 BCE.

Some think that there was a legend among Eastern nations that a star, a king, would arise in Israel, as it had been predicted by a pagan astrologer, Balaam, who is mentioned in the Bible (see Nm 24:17). The Old Testament, which had been translated into Greek 200 years previously, might have been well known outside Jewish circles. The Magi ask for the "King of the Jews," a title that Saint Matthew places on the lips of pagans, since the Jews would have spoken of the "King of Israel."

The star is said to have guided the Magi only from Jerusalem to Bethlehem. For this reason the Magi went to the logical place where a king should be born—the royal residence in Jerusalem. The entire city, together with Herod, was filled with alarm at the news of a newborn king; Herod had just eliminated and assassinated hundreds of people whom he suspected of trying to get rid of him to capture power.

The star stopped over the house where the Child was; time had passed since the crowding during the census ordained by the Roman emperor. In the house, the Magi saw the mother and the Child (Saint Joseph was invisible?) because they looked at them with faith. They adored the Child. Saint Matthew always links the Child and his mother (see Mt 2:11, 13, 14, 20, 21) because for the evangelist the Child belongs in the arms of his mother. After the Magi adored the Child, Herod is no longer given the title of "king"; Jesus will be the only king.

As time passed, Christians adorned this beautiful Gospel story with legends. Saint Matthew does not speak of kings, but since in the psalms it was announced that the Messiah would be adored by kings and that they would offer gold and incense (see Psalm 72:10–11), popular piety gave them the title of the Three Kings. Since Saint Matthew speaks of three gifts offered to the Child, people thought of three offerers, although in ancient art sometimes up to twelve Magi were depicted. Another dimension of the popular legend has been the attribution of various races to the Magi (white, black, and Oriental), since they were to represent all of humanity adoring Christ. Names were also given to the Magi: Melchior, Gaspar, and Balthasar. The legend ends by reporting that the Magi went back to their countries where they gave witness to Christ and because of it, they suffered martyrdom; their remains are venerated in the Cathedral of Cologne in Germany.

24. Is it possible that King Herod really killed the children of Bethlehem?

Some authors think that Saint Matthew is drawing a parallel in speaking of the killing of the children in Bethlehem with the killing of children in Egypt during the time of Moses, when Israel was born as a people. Others think that if the killing of the children would have been a historical event, it would have been mentioned by the historians of that time since they speak of the life and the crimes of the reign of King Herod.

Nevertheless, the killing of the children is very much in accord with what is known of Herod, but since it dealt with the death of just less than a hundred unimportant children, historians do not mention it. "Herod the Great" was great in many ways: he was a great warrior, a great constructor of monuments and temples (in Jerusalem and in other cities), a man of great generosity during a famine among the people, and especially great in his revenges, hatred, and murders.

In addition to killing his favorite wife (he had seven other wives), he killed three of his children and several relatives; he also killed three hundred military officers who had been accused of scheming with two of his older sons. Toward the end of his life, Herod killed several hundred Pharisees who plotted against him because he was not of the Jewish race. According to historians, about six thousand Pharisees convinced the king's cook, one of his eunuchs, to kill Herod by giving him a poisoned steak. Herod, who suspected everything and everyone, had the meat given to one of his dogs; the dog had convulsions and died. Herod had the eunuch tortured and learned that the Pharisees had promised the eunuch that after the death of Herod the long-awaited king and Messiah, sent by God, would be coming. This king would reward the eunuch by healing him from his sexual deficiency so that he would be able to have children and he would be held in high honor. The poor man believed the

Pharisees, but the plot failed. Herod had all the leaders of the plot put to death, crucifying them around the city of Jerusalem.

When he was old and sickly, Herod believed that there were too many people interested in his death. He saw plots and dangers among them, even from his own children. It is not surprising, then, that the arrival of the Magi asking for a newborn King of the Jews would be a cause for alarm both for Herod and for the whole city of Jerusalem (see Mt 2:3); people were afraid of new revenge and killing from the king. To kill the children of Bethlehem was something trivial for such a cruel king.

Since Bethlehem was just a little town with around 2,000 inhabitants and the king ordered the killing of only boys, not girls, the number of children slaughtered must have been around fifty.

25. What is the meaning of the temptations of Jesus in the Gospel of Matthew (4:1–11)?

The temptations of Jesus in Matthew's Gospel look back at the temptations of Israel during the exodus from Egypt and look ahead to the temptations that Christians, the New Israel of God, will suffer. Jesus is the model for those who will struggle against Satan; like Jesus, they will triumph. But Christians also must pray not to be led into temptation (see Mt 6:13), and they will have to be alert and persevering in prayer so that they will not fall into temptation, since the spirit is strong and the flesh is weak (see Mt 26:41).

In the synoptic Gospels, the temptations of Jesus are in continuity with the baptism of Jesus. He is the first representative of the New Israel, who passes through the water (of the Jordan River, just as the Israelites had passed through the Red Sea) to go into the desert to suffer temptation. The temptations are similar: manna and bread, the vision of the land by Moses from Mount Nebo and the vision of Jesus of the kingdoms of the world (see Deut 32:48–49). Jesus conquers where the Old Israel failed.

The New Israel is tempted in Jesus and with Jesus; the answers of Jesus to the devil are taken from the trials of Israel in the desert (see Dt 6:13,16; 8:3). At its origins, the New Israel is reliving the experiences of the people of the Old Testament. The temptations of Jesus are a mystery that also impressed the writers of the New Testament (see Heb 2:18; 4:15).

The devil tempts Jesus, asking him to prove that he is the Son of God, as it had been revealed in his baptism at the Jordan River (see Mt

3:17). Jesus will show who he is during his public ministry, but not in the terms suggested by the devil. The temptations of the devil invite Jesus to give way to selfishness without limit:

1. In the first temptation, after fasting forty days, the hungry Jesus is asked to take care of his health, making use of his powers and talents to remedy his own weakness, since charity begins at home. Jesus answers that there are more important needs than those of the body. To follow the plans and desires of God is most important, although it sometimes demands sacrifices.
2. In the second temptation, Jesus is asked to jump from a temple height within sight of everyone so that God will send his angels to rescue him. This temptation is common for people who lack elementary prudence and get into all sorts of problems; they want God to come to save them. One must not pretend to have God at the service of one's whims.
3. In the third temptation, it is suggested to Jesus that there is a way to make everyone serve him. All of us like to be served. But Jesus did not come to be served but to serve and give his life in sacrifice for the many (see Mt 20:28). Jesus left us the example. We must adore and serve only God.

Jesus had similar temptations during his public ministry when the Pharisees asked him to perform miracles just to show off and when they asked him questions just to entrap him.

26. What is the importance of the Beatitudes, which have been called the *Magna Carta* of the kingdom of God (Mt 5:1-12)?

The Beatitudes are critically important in the Gospel of Matthew, not only because of their contents but also by reason of their placement in the structure of the Gospel (see Mt 5:1-12). The Beatitudes are at the beginning of the first great discourse of Jesus, telling us that the citizens of God's kingdom are the poor and the needy. At the end of the last discourse, the eschatological announcement of the consummation of the kingdom, we hear the narration of the Last Judgment (see Mt 25:31-46). There we find that those who share their wealth and take sides with the needy are also admitted into the kingdom.

The Beatitudes of Matthew are presented with a literary inclusion that opens and closes the narration:

Blessed are the poor in spirit,
for theirs is the kingdom of heaven.
Blessed are those who are persecuted for righteousness' sake,
for theirs is the kingdom of heaven.

Between the first and the last Beatitudes we find the list of the kinds of people who, because of who they are or what they do, already belong in the kingdom of heaven: the meek and disposed, those who mourn, those who hunger and thirst for righteousness, the merciful, those pure in heart, and those who work for peace.

There are some who think that Jesus, like some Jews of his time, thought that the end of the present age was very near and that the kingdom of God was to bring an inversion of values; the poor and the afflicted needed patience because their condition was going to be changed radically by God. In the new order of things, the first would be last and the last would become first (see Mt 19:30; 20:16). It is more probable that Matthew, writing for Jews converted from Judaism, saw them as persecuted for their new faith, even by their own family; they suffered imprisonment and all kinds of difficulties; they had to wait patiently for God's salvation, because the Lord was not going to abandon his own. This was especially the case for those included in the ninth and last beatitude—Christians who suffered persecution because of their active participation in propagating the new faith in Jesus.

27. What is the basic message of the first discourse of Jesus, of the Sermon on the Mount (Mt 5—7)?

The Sermon on the Mount solemnly introduces the new attitudes and laws of God's kingdom. It is centered in two key verses around which the whole sermon is built:

1. Do not think that I have come to abolish the law or the prophets; I have come not to abolish but to fulfill (Mt 5:17).
2. For I tell you, unless your righteousness exceeds that of the scribes and Pharisees, you will never enter the kingdom of heaven (Mt 5:20).

Verse 17 presents the Christian attitude toward the Law of Moses and the relationship of the New Israel to the Old; it is explained through examples in the first half of the sermon: One should not kill; one should not even get angry and do harm to others; adultery included evil desires toward another woman; divorce is now forbidden; one should not swear, but tell the truth always; the law of an eye for an eye must give way to forgiveness and generosity; one must not hate even one's enemies, since Christian love must be universal, just like that of the heavenly Father.

Verse 5:20 sets an ideal of holiness much higher than the one that was common among pious persons of the time: When one gives alms, prays, or fasts, the only thing that counts is to be guided by a correct intention toward God our Father. One must not do good actions to be seen by people but just to please the heavenly Father who sees everything. The thoughts and actions of the believer must always be guided by his faith, respect, and love for the will of the Father. The end of the sermon emphasizes that good intentions are not good enough, because a good Christian is not just one who speaks or thinks well; a good Christian is the one who acts and lives according to his Christian faith and values.

28. The Our Father of Saint Matthew is different from the one found in Saint Luke's Gospel. Which is the version actually used by Jesus?

Comparing both versions of the Our Father easily shows the differences between the two:

MATTHEW 6:9–13	LUKE 11:2–4
Our Father in heaven,	Father,
hallowed be your name.	hallowed be your name
Your kingdom come.	Your kingdom come
Your will be done, on earth	
as it is in heaven.	
Give us this day our daily bread.	Give us each day our daily bread
And forgive us our debts,	And forgive us our sins,
as we also have forgiven	for we ourselves forgive everyone
our debtors.	indebted to us.
And do not bring us	And do not bring us
to the time of trial,	to the time of trial.
but rescue us from the evil one.	

The text of Saint Luke is shorter and probably older. Initially, the Our Father probably was recited in the Christian communities without a fixed formula; it expressed the basic attitudes necessary for Christian life. In some communities, since early times, the Our Father concluded with the formula "For the kingdom and the power and the glory are yours, now and forever, Lord." This formula is not included in the inspired text.

Saint Matthew begins addressing God with a longer and Jewish formula; he includes seven petitions, more in agreement with the mentality and the numbers favored by Jews. Saint Luke has only five petitions. The sanctification of the name of God is one of the duties stressed in the Old Testament and in many Jewish prayers. The coming of God's kingdom was a fervent desire of the Jews in the time of Jesus, and it was often included in their prayers. "Your will be done" is very much in agreement with the theology of Saint Matthew on the importance of obedience to God. The "daily bread" can be referred to the Eucharist, the bread that feeds the believers, although it may be a reference to the manna of the desert, the daily bread that God gave to his people during the Exodus from Egypt (see Ex 16:13–21).

Throughout the New Testament, and in the Gospel of Saint Matthew more than in other texts, the forgiveness of sins is a basic duty for Christians. Christians are called to be channels of God's forgiveness. They are those who know they have been forgiven by God and because of that they forgive each other. At the end of the Our Father, Saint Matthew stresses again the duty of forgiveness, as he does again at the end of chapter 18. The temptation that we must overcome is principally the eschatological temptation through which the Evil One will try to take away the elect.

29. Why does Saint Matthew condemn the Pharisees so harshly?

Some people ask why Saint Matthew, more than any other Gospel, is so insistent in his accusations and denunciations against the Pharisees, especially since the Pharisees who opposed Jesus had already died during the destruction of Jerusalem by the Romans. Several answers are possible:

- The Pharisees continued to be the Jewish group that actively opposed the newborn church. The Pharisees were the most important Jewish group after the destruction of Jerusalem and for a time directed the Jewish survivors from the catastrophe.

- Saint Matthew condemns the Pharisees for their heartless legalism, their pride, and hypocrisy. They thought more of themselves than of God and neighbor. Saint Luke also condemns their pride, as he describes them in the parable of the Pharisee and the tax collector (see Lk 18:9–14).

- It is also possible that Saint Matthew had in mind a new breed of Pharisees that could come up in the Christian community—people who would have the same attitudes and values of the old Pharisees who opposed Jesus and who consider themselves better than others. This type of person may come up at any time, since, as the Spanish proverb says, "a bad weed never dies."

30. Was the Sermon on Parables pronounced by Jesus or was it composed by Saint Matthew (Mt 13:1–52)?

The Sermon on Parables (Matthew 13) is a composition by the evangelist who compiled the teachings of Jesus. Saint Matthew, using a series of stories narrated by Jesus, wants to present the process of development of the kingdom of God, from its beginning to its consummation. The picture presented by Matthew is very suggestive: Jesus preaches from the boat while the people sit on the lakeshore.

We must not think that we have here the Day of the Parables, as it is presented by some authors. Jesus probably used parables on a daily basis as the opportunity arose. This collection of seven parables has been placed by Saint Matthew at the center of the five discourses of Jesus to clarify the message on the kingdom of God. Some of this material is also found in the Gospel of Mark.

Parables are frequently stories or narrations taken from rural life, from nature, or from some activity of the people. Their purpose is to teach religious truths, but they require reflection to be understood and accepted; teaching through stories was a more attractive way of presenting a doctrine. Perhaps Saint Matthew wanted to confront a double reality: (1) the lack of faith and the rejection of the message by the Jews, and (2) the reality of the Christian community that was being persecuted because of its fidelity to the message of Jesus.

Saint Matthew offers as a reason for the parables the fulfillment of the prophecies about the incredulity of the Jewish people. Sometimes we say the opposite of what we mean to call people to reflect on what they are hearing—as the Spanish proverb states, "I tell you the contrary, so that you will better understand."

Saint Matthew thinks of the Christian community for whom he writes the Gospel. The parables contain lessons that the Christian readers must apply to their lives and behavior, as indicated in the following text:

1. *The parable of the sower* (see Mt 13:1–23). This is the best-known parable in Matthew's Gospel. It was easy for the early Christian communities to seek explanations of why the Jews, and some Christians, were not receiving the message of Jesus and not "producing fruit." It was easy to understand that others would be the "bad soil" of which the parable speaks, and faithful followers of Christ would see themselves as the good soil. Each of us can have hearts of stone and our own personal "thorns" that prevent us from producing fruit. We must continually strive to change all the "soil" of our heart into a productive plot, eliminating the distractions, stones, and thorns that we sometimes harbor for others. When a field is planted with seed, its gradually changes, becoming a plush, green sight pleasant to behold. Similarly, a person guided by the Gospel's doctrine of love and sacrifice gradually becomes more attractive and pleasant.

2. *The parable of the good seed* that grows among the weeds (see Mt 13:24–30) calls the members of the Christian community to live in peace, patience, and tolerance, either with the Jews or with other members of the community who have their own personal faults and sins. God will take care of judging each one according to his or her merits.

3. *The twin parables of the mustard seed and the leaven (yeast)* (see Mt 3:31–33) highlight the contrast between the humble beginnings of the Christian community and the future that God prepares for it. Some may consider the parable of the mustard seed a slight exaggeration, since the mustard "tree" (more resembling a large bush) did not usually grow beyond twelve feet. Similarly, others see exaggeration in the parable of the leaven, since three measures of flour could produce bread to feed a hundred people; conversely,

some see in the three leavened loaves an allusion to the three loaves Mary probably made every week for the Holy Family; Jesus would be taking this parable from his own home experience.

4. *The twin parables of the treasure and the pearl* (see Mt 13:44–46) invite us to sacrifice everything for the sake of the kingdom. The most precious things are those God has offered and revealed to us.

5. *The parable of the net that gathers fish of every kind* (see Mt 13:47) again stresses the idea that a final or definitive judgment awaits everyone at the end of time. In this life we are called to grow in faith and love. God expects much fruit from us, and we must respond to Him.

31. According to Matthew's Gospel, how should leadership be exercised in the Church (Mt 18:1–36)?

Chapter 18 of Matthew's Gospel is considered by some commentators as a program for the life of the Christian community, dealing with the problems that arise in daily relationships. Some see it as a series of instructions directed particularly to the disciples as leaders of the Christian community.

If Jesus' discourse is directed to the apostles as leaders of the community, what should their priorities be and how must they address problems and difficulties? Chapter 18 has two distinct sections. The first section (vv. 1–14) repeats the word *child* (or *little ones*) (vv. 2, 4, 5, 6, 10, 14), giving clear directions for the relationship of the leaders with the humble and simple members of the community.

The first quality of an authentic Christian leader should be his or her humility in relationship to the simple or ordinary faithful. The leaders should be like children, like persons at the service of others, without rights, and without considering themselves important. Leaders also should be very sensitive to the weaker members of the community, embracing responsibility for their spiritual well-being. Leaders should guide first by example, so that no one will be scandalized or lost. This first part of the discourse closes with the Parable of the Lost Sheep (vv. 10–14), through which Christian leaders are asked to see to it that no one be lost, and if anyone strays from the community, leaders must seek them and convince them to return. The sheep must be precious to the leaders because they are precious also to God.

The second part of the discourse (vv. 15–35) deals with the attitude of leaders toward the other members of the community (*brothers, sisters,* or *others; see* vv. 15, 21, 35) who cause difficulties in the community. A humble leader will not feel offended when the erring member does not accept fraternal correction or disrespects the community. That person will need extra vigilance to be reconverted and return fully as a member of the community. The text does not deal with exclusion or excommunication of the sinner, since the sheep are all precious and must be kept within the fold of the flock at all costs. There will always be good and bad members within the community, as suggested in the Parable of the Weeds; the members must live together even if the relationship with some members will not always be the same as with other members.

Above all, the leader must be a person who knows how to forgive. Saint Peter, who already was considered a leader of the group, might have felt generous in his statement that he forgives up to seven times. A person in a high leadership position may become conscious of his or her importance and esteem and might be more easily offended because others do not hold him or her in the same esteem. The Christian leader must not become the center of his or her preoccupations, interests, and ministry. The leader should think only of Jesus and of how to bring others to Jesus, helping them grow in their faith. Forgiveness without limits is a prerequisite for authentic and fruitful Christian leadership.

The second part of the discourse also ends with a parable, stressing the duty of forgiveness, since the members of the Christian community must see themselves as sinners who have been forgiven by God and who know how to forgive each other.

32. What did Saint Matthew expect the end of the world and the Final Judgment to be like (Mt 24–25)?

The destruction of Jerusalem and the Temple dealt a death blow for the hopes of many Jews who lived during the time of Saint Matthew. Many believed that the end of the world was at hand. Christians who had been expecting a Second Coming of Jesus saw that it was being delayed, and it was most important to be ready for whenever it might happen.

For more than thirty years, Christians had suffered from discrimination, persecutions, insecurity, wars, and confusion. The community had to deepen its faith and continue preaching the Gospel until the end of time. Saint Matthew did not like his community to live in anguish because of their present situation. The Second Coming of Jesus was to happen when the life of people would be occupied in ordinary chores and work; it would come as a big surprise amidst everyday activity. Christians should know that the goal of Jesus' coming was to save his elect; they were to live at peace and with confidence, attentive to their duties of mutual service.

Saint Matthew, following the style of apocalyptic writers, describes the Second Coming of Jesus along the lines of visits of imperial authorities to the region. Their coming was announced beforehand, messengers were sent ahead to prepare the last details for the visit, and the sound of a trumpet announced the arrival of the authority figure. Everyone was expected to respond and come to welcome the arrival. Lack of preparation was unforgivable and could be punished severely. Saint Matthew also uses images from the prophets, describing the cosmic signs that would accompany the coming of the Lord to judge his people and the nations.

The description of the Last Judgment is generally considered a parable of the consequences of the personal decision to follow (or not to follow) the teachings of Jesus. After the three parables on vigilance (the servant, the ten virgins, and the talents), the Last Judgment is a culminating parable. Everyone must be ready to give an account of one's conduct.

The theology of Saint Matthew seems to reflect the beliefs of Jews of his time. Many expected a double judgment at the end of time: one for the tribes of Israel and another for pagan nations. The judgment of the tribes of Israel was to be done by Jesus in association with the twelve apostles seated on twelve thrones. The judgment of pagan nations would be done by Jesus alone, making those nations responsible for their response to the message of Jesus, who identifies himself with the needy.

It is more probable that Saint Matthew was thinking not so much of what would happen to the members of his community at the end of time but rather of what was already happening in his own time. The Last Judgment could be a process that was happening all throughout history. The kingdom of God is always arriving, and everyone has the opportunity and the duty to become part of it. The messengers of the kingdom, the apostles of that time, were the poor and the hungry, the thirsty, the pilgrims, and the imprisoned. A response toward them and their mission in favor of the Gospel made people members of the kingdom; those who did not receive or help the messengers of the kingdom were condemning themselves. Even now the judgment continues: those who open themselves to the needy are already Christian at heart; those who close themselves to others exclude themselves from the kingdom, even if they had been invited and considered themselves good Christians. To those Jesus will say that he does not know them (see Mt 25:12), that they will remain outside in the darkness where they belong.

33. What is Peter's role in the church according to Matthew's Gospel?

Saint Peter has a distinguished role in each of the four Gospels, but it is in Matthew's Gospel that Peter's mission is detailed. Peter has been chosen by a special providence from God to be the shepherd of the flock to whom Jesus will entrust his sheep (see Mt 16:13–20). Peter is to be like a great rabbi of the community, with authority to interpret the new law and power to tie and to untie. He has the power of the keys to open and close the door to those who wish to enter into the kingdom.

Although he was chosen by God, Saint Peter had to discover his own identity and get to know Jesus more fully so that he could understand his own vocation. To the first prediction of the passion by Jesus, Peter responded from a purely human perspective because he did not see the need or the significance of the cross of Jesus. Jesus *had* to go to the cross. The disciples, starting with Peter, also had to be ready to accept the cross and sacrifice in their own lives (see Mt 16:21–23).

Peter's faith grew gradually. His attempt to walk on water reveals a mixture of faith and doubt that still governed his faith and trust in Jesus (see Mt 14:24–34).

The second prediction of the passion of Jesus is followed by another story in which Peter is the agent, this time united intimately with Jesus. The Lord orders Peter to catch a fish that will have a coin in its mouth; with that coin, Peter will pay the temple tax for Jesus and for himself. This narration, found only in the Gospel of Matthew, shows the communion that exists between Peter and Jesus—in a way, both are going to be like the two sides of the same coin in the pastoral care of the flock of the Father (see Mt 17:22–27).

34. Which of the seven last words of Jesus on the cross are found in Matthew's Gospel (Mt 27:32–56)?

The seven last words of Jesus on the cross are nothing more than a pastoral arrangement, very useful for meditation on the sacrifice of Jesus for our sins. For Hispanics, the seven last words are an important part of Good Friday services. These seven last words are not all found in single Gospel story. Each evangelist has chosen to put in the lips of Jesus some words that, in his opinion, better expressed the last will and testament of Jesus at the end of his life.

Saint Luke emphasizes the words of forgiveness, the conversion and salvation of the Good Thief, and the trust of Jesus at the moment of his death (see Lk 23:34–46). Saint John recalls the mission of Mary after the passion, the thirst of Jesus, and the fulfillment of his work (see Jn 19:26–27, 28, 30).

Saint Matthew, together with Saint Mark, places on the lips of Jesus only one of the seven last words, the quotation from Psalm 22: "My God, my God, why have you forsaken me?" Some commentators see in this a desperate cry of Jesus, who drank the bitter chalice until the last drop. Others think that the evangelist wants us to think that while on the cross Jesus recited the entire prayer of this psalm. Then, in the midst of his torments, Jesus lived a holy hour of prayer in which he saw the actions of his persecutors in light of the prophecies, which end with an affirmation of hope in what the Father was doing through Jesus for the salvation of the world. Either of these two views has value in moving the hearts of Christians to greater love for our Redeemer.

35. According to Matthew, where is Jesus now and where can he be found (Mt 28:16–20)?

This question about where Jesus is, or can be found by Christians, is answered differently in each of the four Gospels since each evangelist offers the teaching he considered most important for his community. Even now, we can recall the answer taught in our youth in the old catechism: "Jesus is in heaven and on earth, everywhere, and specially in the Blessed Sacrament of the altar...."

At the beginning (Mt 1:23) and at the end (28:20) of his Gospel, Matthew presents Jesus as the *God-with-us* who is with us until the end of the world, never leaving us alone. Jesus also identifies himself with the leaders and the members of the church, especially when they gather together in prayer to make decisions about those who are in error (see Mt 18:20).

Jesus also identifies himself with his apostles and missionaries who bring the Gospel to the nations; those who receive them also are receiving Jesus who sends them (see Mt 10:40). Jesus' identification of himself with the poor and the needy in the narration of the Last Judgment is well known: "What you did to the least of my brothers, you did it to me" (Mt 25:40).

3

THE GOSPEL
OF SAINT MARK

36. Who was Mark? When and where did he write his Gospel?

According to church tradition, Saint Mark is the John Mark named in
The Acts of the Apostles whose mother had a house in Jerusalem, where
the members of the newborn church gathered (see Acts 12:12–14).

Mark was the cousin or nephew of Saint Barnabas (see Col 4:10); they
traveled together (see Acts 12:45). Later Mark was the cause of the separa-
tion between Saint Paul and Barnabas (see Acts 15:37–39). Saint Mark must
have reconciled with Saint Paul and collaborated with him (see 2 Tim 4:11);
he accompanied Saint Paul during his imprisonment at Rome (Phil 24).

In the First Letter of Saint Peter, Mark is called *son* by this apostle (see
5:13). In about AD 135, the ecclesiastical writer Papias calls Saint Mark
"the interpreter of Peter." The apostle who had been a fisherman in Galilee
may not have found it easy to learn Greek and Latin; because of this he
must have needed an interpreter or translator for his preaching.

Church tradition also states that Saint Mark wrote his Gospel in Rome
after the martyrdom of Saints Peter and Paul. Some portions of Mark's Gospel seem to reflect the theology of Saint Paul's letters. There are also signs
of the influence of the Latin language on the Greek text of the Gospel.

It is possible that the story found in Saint Mark's Gospel about the
young man who ran away naked during the arrest of Jesus at the beginning of the passion might be a way of telling the readers that in his youth
Saint Mark had some direct contact with the Lord.

37. What is the purpose or aim of the Gospel of Saint Mark?

According to church tradition, Saint Mark wrote what he remembered
of the preaching of his teacher, after the death of Saint Peter. He wrote

as best as he could, without order. Nevertheless, a careful analysis of this Gospel shows some sections are very well thought out and in good order. Some narrations, such as the double multiplication of the bread, suggest that Saint Mark had access to some sources and information about which we have little knowledge.

From the beginning of this Gospel, it is easy to see that Saint Mark writes to highlight the powers of Jesus. Saint Mark probably had in mind the power of the Roman emperor Nero, who had killed the two great apostles and seemed bent on crushing the new faith. With Jesus on their side, Christians could resist and oppose the emperor. The key to Jesus' powers and those of Christians is faith and prayer. Saint Mark underscores the powers of Jesus in several passages (see Mk 1:27, 40; 2:1–12, 28; 4:41, 5:3–4, 42; 8:4; 9:29).

Saint Mark presents Jesus as the Messiah, the powerful Savior announced by the prophets and expected by the Jews. Jesus is also the Son of the Father who will voluntarily sacrifice himself so that we might become sons and daughters of the Father.

38. What is the general structure of Saint Mark's Gospel?

The opening verse of the Gospel provides us a general overview of book. It is the good news about Jesus, who is the expected Messiah and the Son of God.

This first verse points to the division of the Gospel into two parts: those dealing with Jesus the Messiah and Jesus as the Son of God.

FIRST PART (Mk 1:1—8:30)	SECOND PART (Mk 8:31—16:20)
Jesus the Messiah	Jesus the Son
Confession of Peter (8:29)	Confession of the centurion (15:39)
Jesus and his actions	Jesus and his passion
Many miracles	Few miracles
Jesus with the crowds	Jesus with the disciples
Concrete commandments	Universal commandments
Emphasis on power	Emphasis on service

These two parts of the Gospel, with the marked difference in the activity of Jesus after the confession of Peter and the first prediction of the passion, are reminiscent of Saint John's Gospel. If the first edition of the fourth Gospel is almost contemporary with the Gospel of Mark, the change of the activity of Jesus could be associated with the Galilean crisis, after which Jesus centers his teachings and ministry on the Twelve, in preparation of his passion. In Saint John's Gospel, after the sermon on the Bread of Life, many Jews and even many of his disciples abandoned Jesus because they could not accept his doctrine (see Jn 6:66–71).

The order of Mark's Gospel is similar to the one in the other two synoptic Gospels: introduction of the ministry; baptism in the Jordan River; ministry in Galilee; travels through the region of Tyre, Sidon, Decapolis, and Caesarea Philippi; ascent to Jerusalem through Perea and Jericho; passion and resurrection.

A special characteristic of the Gospel of Saint Mark is the messianic secret. Mark repeats several times that Jesus ordered the witnesses of his miracles to keep them secret and not publicize them. Some authors think that Mark was trying to answer a possible objection of those who did not believe: If Jesus performed so many miracles, why did the Jews not believe in him? Mark offers in response that although Jesus performed many miracles, he did not exploit them for propaganda about himself.

39. What are the key teachings of Mark's Gospel?

From the very first verse Saint Mark announces two key teachings about Jesus: He is the Messiah and he is the Son of God.

1. Jesus is the expected Messiah, the powerful savior who with his marvelous actions would destroy the powers of Satan and save those oppressed by illnesses and sufferings. No one, and nothing, can resist the powers of Jesus—neither the threats of the Jews nor the persecution of Emperor Nero, who happened to be the most powerful man in the world of that time.

2. Jesus is also the Son of God, the one who will save through his sufferings and sacrifice, accepted willingly, and who will transform his disciples and even the whole world.

3. The disciples, following the example and the way of Jesus, will accept sacrifice as part of their lives through humble service to others. The passion of Jesus must be assimilated by the disciples as a consequence of their association with Jesus.

4. The disciples will continue the ministry of Jesus healing the sick, casting out demons, and overcoming evil.

5.   The kingdom of God has arrived with the preaching of the Gospel; it demands repentance and new attitudes from anyone who is to belong to it.

40. Why does Saint Mark emphasize the powers of Jesus so strongly?

Saint Mark wants to convince his readers that the only one who has all power over hearts, and over the realm of the material and the spiritual, is Jesus. The Roman emperor Nero had very limited powers. Jesus' powers are not military or political; they are spiritual and divine.

To emphasize the powers of Jesus, the evangelist has ordered the first seven stories of his Gospel in a symmetrical pattern so that they correspond among themselves as follows:

Mk 1:16–20 Vocation: Near the lake, saw, follow, left, followed, called FISHERMEN
> **Mk 1:21–28 Spiritual power:** Capernaum, teaching with authority, unclean spirit, teaching with authority
>> **Mk 1:29–34 Healing of the sick:** Fever and illnesses
>> **Mk 1:35–39 The prayer of Jesus**
>> **Mk 1:40–45 Healing of a leper:** A most-feared illness
> **Mk 2:1–12 Spiritual power:** Capernaum, power and authority to forgive sins
Mk 2:13–17 Vocation: Near the lake, saw, follow, followed, to call SINNERS

The powers revealed in the last three stories, although of the same type as the first three stories, overflow and are more intense.

We can see the power of Jesus over the hearts of the disciples, simple fishermen, who leave their daily chores to become followers of Jesus. It is not surprising that they left everything, since the work of fishermen was difficult, at times dangerous, and not always productive. Peter left his boat, but he must have left it well tied up, for whenever Jesus needed a boat, Peter's was always at hand. In the parallel narration, the response of Levi is much deeper and radical than that of Peter; Levi leaves everything—the money and the job—to follow Jesus; he will not be able to go back to his old job.

The healing of the fever of the mother-in-law of Peter, and of the sick of the town, was not so spectacular in an area where there were other faith healers and places of healing (in Jerusalem there was the pool of Bethzatha, of which Saint John speaks in 5:1–4), but the healing of a leper was something unheard of, almost equivalent to a resurrection and new life.

The expulsion of the demon in the synagogue, even if seems striking because of its speed, was something the Jews sometimes did with great effort and danger (see Acts 19:13–16). But the forgiveness of sins was such a divine power that no human person could claim it.

In the middle of these narrations of Jesus' powers, the evangelist tells us that Jesus retired to a quiet, lonely place where he was at prayer (the Greek imperfect tense implies some length of time spent in prayer). Prayer is the key and center of the powers of Jesus and of the powers of a Christian. Prayer places Jesus on the side of the Christians so that in the future they will not have to fear Emperor Nero or any other power of this world.

Even in our own times, the powers of Jesus are still the same. It is always good to reflect on how Jesus exercises these powers in our communities: when persons renounce material things, share their goods, when demons and vices are conquered, when people forgive, and when physical and spiritual healings take place.

41. What is special in the vocation of the disciples in the Gospel of Mark (Mk 3:13–19)?

The narrations of the vocations of the disciples in the Gospels of saints Mark and Matthew have clear similarities and differences:

MK 3:13–15	MT 10:1
He went up the mountain and called to him those whom he wanted, and they came to him. And he appointed twelve, whom he also named apostles, to be with him, and to be sent out to proclaim the message, and to have authority to cast out demons.	Then Jesus summoned his twelve disciples and gave them authority over unclean spirits, to cast them out, and to cure every disease and every sickness.

For Saint Matthew, the disciples are principally the laborers who must gather the abundant harvest; the crowds are like sheep without a shepherd, and the harvest is plentiful but the laborers few (see Mt 9:35–38). For Saint Mark, the disciples are called in the first place to be with Jesus, as his friends and confidants. Jesus seeks friends to whom he can open his heart; he does not want servants or slaves. Living with Jesus will prepare the disciples so that later they will be sent as missionaries to preach and heal in the name of Jesus (see Mk 6:7–13).

42. What special powers does Mark attribute to Jesus?

In question 40, we saw the powers of Jesus that directly affected the lives and the hearts of the people. At the end of chapter 4 (see Mk 4:35–41) and throughout chapter 5, Saint Mark presents powers of Jesus that associate him more directly with the divine: power over the sea and its storms, over demons, and over death itself.

The calming of the storm (see 4:35–41) fills the disciples with religious admiration. As fishermen, they know well the power of the sea and its cycles. Jews also associated the sea with monsters and evil powers, but nothing can offer resistance to Jesus' power.

The possessed man of Jerash (see 5:3–14), freed by Jesus from a legion of devils whom neither chains nor fetters could restrain, experiences the liberating power of Jesus.

Two women come in contact with the power of Jesus when he overcomes a long sickness, and even death. Some of the Christians for whom Saint Mark wrote were threatened with death by the power of Rome. They could be assured that the power of Jesus would restore them and bring them to an eternal life.

43. How many times did Jesus multiply the bread—once or twice?

Saint Mark narrates two multiplications of the bread. He probably just offers two versions of the same miracle—one from a Jewish tradition and the other from a pagan tradition. The second narration of the miracle, the one narrated in all the Gospels, extends the meaning of the miracle to new readers, with Jesus inviting *everyone* to receive his gifts. All are called to become members of the new people of God and to participate in the messianic banquet. Saints Luke and John speak of only one multiplication of the bread.

In Matthew's Gospel (9:36–37), when the crowds were like sheep without a shepherd, Jesus sent his disciples to preach. Saint Mark relates that at first the hungry crowd is given the word of Jesus, and then they are given the food for the body in the first multiplication (Mt 6:34–45).

The interesting similarities and the slight differences are worth noting:

Mt 6:34–45	Mk 8:1–10
Jesus is saddened because the people are like sheep without a shepherd.	Jesus feels compassion because the people have no food, and if he were to send them away, they would faint along the way.
The disciples take the initiative.	Jesus takes the initiative.
200 denari are needed.	
They have five loaves and two fish.	They have seven loaves and some fish.
Jesus orders the people to sit on the green grass, in groups of hundreds and fifties (as in the Exodus).	Jesus orders the people to sit on the ground.
He blessed the bread and broke it, and gave it to the disciples to serve the people.	He took the seven loaves, gave thanks, broke them, and gave them to the disciples to serve the people.
And he distributed the fish among all and all ate and were satisfied.	He blessed the fish and ordered that they be distributed.
Twelve baskets of leftovers.	Seven baskets of leftovers.
They were about 5,000.	They were about 4,000.
Afterward Jesus walks on the water.	In the boat, Jesus questions the faith and the memory of the blind disciples.

Most biblical scholars think that Saint Mark found in his sources two narrations of the same miracle. The first one was presented for Christians converted from Judaism; this narration echoes the Exodus narrative and the story of the manna in the desert. The leftover manna fills twelve baskets, a quantity sufficient to feed the New Israel, which Jesus comes to gather.

The second narration apparently is from a group of Christians converted from paganism. The evangelist adds that some of the people had come *from afar*, a phrase that ordinarily refers to pagans.

44. What is the significance of the disciples' ignorance, which Saint Mark seems to emphasize (Mk 8:14–21)?

After the two multiplications of the bread, Saint Mark stresses the lack of understanding of the disciples. In 6:52, Mark says that the disciples were astounded because they had not understood about the bread, and their hearts (minds) were closed. Jesus had just come to them walking on the water, identifying himself as *I AM*, a name charged with significance. If the theology of Mark has a relationship with that of the Gospel of Saint John, we might suppose this to be a reference to Jesus as the Bread of Life and that it was God who had just fed the people. This association with the Gospel of Saint John is also valid for the dialogue of Jesus with the disciples after the second multiplication of the bread. The disciples ignored something very basic: that they had only one loaf of bread in the boat with them (see Mk 8:14). In both instances, the ignorance of the disciples may imply a eucharistic dimension of the miracle, pointing toward the sermon on the Bread of Life in Saint John's Gospel.

Saint Mark underscores the lack of eucharistic intelligence of the miracle, pointing out that the Pharisees had come to Jesus asking for a sign, the same thing the crowd was asking in John's Gospel after they had witnessed the multiplication miracle (see Jn 6:30).

The disciples' lack of understanding is emphasized by means of seven questions that the evangelist places in the lips of Jesus; the first and the last questions are identical: "Do you still not understand?" (see Mk 8:17, 21).

The disciples needed miracles to open their eyes (and minds) in order to understand the mission of Jesus, especially in reference to his sacrifice and passion. When we think how the disciples found it difficult to understand and accept the message of Jesus, we too require the same great effort to grow in knowledge and our life of faith. We can almost say that blindness is a dimension of our life of faith; we must not think of ourselves as more intelligent or better disposed than the disciples—we always must grow in our understanding of the teachings of Jesus.

45. What is the special message of the healing of the blind man from Bethsaida (Mk 8:22–26)?

After the second multiplication of the bread, Mark's narratives seem to take on a symbolic meaning. If the multiplication of the bread was associated with the Eucharist, and Jesus was the true Bread they had in the boat, the disciples were so blind that only a miracle could open their minds. This miracle happened in Bethsaida when Jesus opened the eyes of a blind man; the eyes that were really opened with that miracle were the eyes of Peter (Peter and his brother Andrew happened to be from Bethsaida). Because his eyes were opened, in the following narration Saint Peter begins to see (he finally realizes) and confesses that Jesus is the Messiah (see Mk 8:29).

The symbolism of the narration is heightened when we consider that Jesus performs the miracle of the blind man in two stages. The initial healing is partial and incomplete—the blind man sees men walking who look like trees. With the second imposition of hands by Jesus the blind man starts to see everything, clearly and far away. He now has telescopic eyes.

Peter's eyes were opened as were the eyes of the blind man from Bethsaida, but the healing of Peter was also partial. Peter could see that Jesus was the Messiah, but he still could not see farther—that Jesus had to suffer the passion as part of his mission. Peter was still partially blind. The miracle of Bartimaeus, the blind man of Jericho, will open the eyes of Peter and all the disciples immediately before the start of the passion (see Mk 10:46–52).

46. What is the purpose of the predictions of the passion of Jesus in Mark's Gospel (Mk 8:31–33; 9:30–32; 10:32–34)?

In the second part of his Gospel, Mark has arranged the order of its contents so that the sacrifice of Jesus and its implications for the disciples become clearer. The second part also shows how far the disciples were from understanding what Jesus was telling them. We find the following order:

1. Prediction of the passion: Mk 8:31; 9:31; 10:32–34
2. Lack of understanding by Peter and the other disciples: Mk 8:32–33; 9:32; 10:35–41

3. Teachings of Jesus on the need of sacrificial service:
    Mk 8:34—9:20; 9:33—10:31; 10:42–45

The three predictions of the passion are followed by the misunderstandings of the disciples with additional teachings on the significance and the consequences of the sacrifice of Jesus for the life of his disciples.

The predictions are increasingly more detailed, especially the third one. The lack of understanding by the disciples reaches its climax with the sons of Zebedee; they are thinking of power and glory while Jesus speaks of service and sacrifice. The teachings of Jesus follow a gradual development. After the first prediction, the disciples are invited to sacrifice while following Jesus. After the second prediction, they are invited to humility, inclusiveness, sacrifice, and renunciation of material things so that they can more faithfully follow Jesus. After the third prediction, once again, humble service is stressed, as well as putting distance from the values of the world. The disciples must be ready to accept even death, just as Jesus has done.

Jesus' instructions conclude with the miracle of the blind man of Jericho who became a disciple and follower of Jesus (see Mk 10:52). Together with the eyes of that blind man, the eyes of all the disciples are finally opened to understand the meaning of the sacrifice of Jesus. The verse following the miracle presents Jesus at the gates of Jerusalem and the passion, near the Mount of Olives (see Mk 11:1).

47. What is the message of the narrative on the sons of Zebedee (Mk 10:35–40)?

Saint Mark presents James and John, the sons of Zebedee, as examples of the great gulf that existed between the thoughts of Jesus and the desires and aspirations of the disciples. Saint Mark states that the two brothers approached Jesus with their petition, while Saint Matthew, with more diplomacy, puts the petition on the lips of their mother. Salome, the mother of the two brothers, may have been the sister of Mary, the mother of Jesus, and thus as the aunt of Jesus, asks for the first places for her two sons.

The two brothers think of power and honors, as well as of the glory of Jesus. On his part, Jesus was thinking of his sacrifice and death. The two disciples are practically asking Jesus for a blank check: "Grant us to sit, one at your right hand and one at your left, in your glory" (Mk 10:37)—in essence saying, "We want you to grant us whatever we ask you." Jesus asks them to identify with himself and his sacrifice, to drink the same chalice as Jesus, and to follow him even unto death.

Many authors believe that both James and John had already been martyred when Saint Mark was writing his Gospel. We know from The Acts of the Apostles that James was the first to suffer martyrdom. Several pious legends exist about the fate of Saint John, but it is also probable that, by the time of the writing of the Gospel, he was also dead. This historical timing points toward an early edition of the fourth Gospel at least in its first format.

48. What are the principal teachings in the passion of Jesus as narrated by Saint Mark (Mk 14—15)?

It is important to remember that the passion of Jesus spoke to the Christians of Saint Mark's time about their own passion that they had suffered in the persecution of Emperor Nero. Some Christians, it seems, suffered because they had been accused by cowardly Christians who were afraid of torture.

Saint Mark presents Jesus as a model for Christians. The sufferings of Jesus, and those of Christians, are in accord with the prophecies and the plans of God. Like Jesus, Christians can be identified with the suffering just ones, who suffer at the hands of sinners, as often described in the psalms. Jesus is betrayed by one of his own, while the others abandon him. Jesus goes to his passion without fear, full of confidence in the Father.

Mark's version of the Last Supper is a paschal meal centered on the institution of the Eucharist (see Mk 14:12–25). The blood of Jesus announces a new covenant, a new testament, of God with humanity. The betrayal of Judas and the foretelling of Peter's denials are in contrast with the voluntary sacrifice of Jesus.

In the Garden of Gethsemani, the prayer of Jesus is his source of strength, just as prayer will be the strength of persecuted Christians (see Mk 14:32–42). Jesus' courage and strength is also in contrast to the weakness of the disciples who fall asleep while Jesus suffers agony and prays. Some have noted the similarities of the description of the agony of Jesus with the text of the Our Father, which is not found in Mark's

Gospel. The evangelist speaks of his Father, the kingdom, doing the Father's will, and falling into temptation (see Mk 14:36–42).

When Jesus was arrested, he accepted his fate as the suffering servant who had accepted the will of God, with total control of the situation. Jesus accepts his death without resorting to violence and self-defense (see Mk 14:43–52).

In the two trials of Jesus (before the Sanhedrin and before Pilate; see Mk 14:53–72—15:1–20), Jesus is the just innocent, falsely accused, who accepts his passion. There is a contrast between the courage and strength of Jesus on one side and the weakness of Peter, as well as the courage and silence of Jesus and the weakness and vacillation of Pilate. Both trials conclude with mockery and insults from the Jewish leaders and the Roman soldiers. Jesus would be the model for Christians falsely accused and punished by Roman authorities.

The narration of the crucifixion raises the question of the time of day when Jesus was actually crucified. Mark states that it happened around nine in the morning (see Mk 15:21–32). The evangelist echoes Psalm 22, a text with which Christian martyrs could identify. The loneliness of Jesus on the cross, betrayed by his own, the silence of the Father, as well as the mockery of the people, were a lesson for Christians in similar situations. If Jesus, as it is possible, recited the entire Psalm 22 on the cross, he would be expressing his feeling of abandonment, as well as a firm confidence that God will have the last word—the cross will end in life and glory. Saint Mark highlights the events that somehow proclaim the innocence of Jesus: the darkness that covered the earth, the tearing of the Temple veil, and the faith confession of the Roman soldier. Only true believers could understand the full significance of these details.

49. What significance does Saint Mark see in the burial and the resurrection of Jesus (Mk 15—16)?

Saint Mark's narrative of the burial and resurrection of Jesus is very brief (see Mk 15:42–47—16:1–8). He emphasizes the fact that the Jesus who really dies is the Jesus who really rose from the dead. He leaves no room for doubt. The women are the witnesses who saw where Jesus was buried and who went on Sunday to the same tomb and found it empty.

All the professions of faith of the ancient church repeat that Jesus *died and was buried*. The women did not expect to find the tomb empty; they had bought perfume to finish the embalming of the body of Jesus. The resurrection was something totally unexpected. The vision of an angel in the sepulcher stresses the occurrence of a miracle. The women react, as would be expected, with a religious fear that leaves them speechless. If the Gospel ended with the fear of the women, there would still be pending questions: *Where is the body of Jesus after his resurrection? Where can believers see him?* Jesus' resurrection announces the future resurrection of those who believe in him, especially if they have accompanied Jesus through a death like his own, through their own martyrdom during the persecution of Emperor Nero.

50. Why is the conclusion of Mark's Gospel so different from the rest of his Gospel (Mk 16:9–20)?

The conclusion of Saint Mark's Gospel was written some time after the rest of the Gospel. The conclusion relates the apparitions of Jesus as narrated in the other Gospels. A redactor, taking the information from the other Gospels, summarizes the apparitions of Jesus, underscoring the lack of understanding of the disciples, a theme stressed by Mark. Other conclusions for Mark's Gospel have been found in some manuscripts. This indicates that from very early times it was believed that the Gospel had not ended originally as it would have been desired or expected.

Modern biblical scholars think that the Gospel originally ended with the religious fear of the women who disobey the command of the angel (see Mk 16:6). Some scholars believe that originally there was another conclusion to the Gospel but it was lost. The actual conclusion (see Mk 16:9–20) was probably written early in the second century since it reveals a knowledge of the other Gospels and The Acts of the Apostles. The literary style and vocabulary of the conclusion differ from the Gospel. This conclusion is found in some of the most widely accepted ancient manuscripts; the Catholic Church accepts it as inspired and canonical, even though it was not written by the same evangelist responsible for the rest of the Gospel.

4

THE GOSPEL OF SAINT LUKE

51. Who is Saint Luke, the author of the third Gospel?

Saint Luke was an admirer and traveling companion of Saint Paul on several of his trips (see Philem 24; Col 4:14; 2 Tim 4:11). Saint Luke was a person of great talent and sensitivity, born and educated in the Greek culture. He knew well the rules of grammar and Greek rhetoric. He also knew the Old Testament well, interpreting it and referring to it often. He even imitated the literary style of the Greek text of the Bible, which was used widely in the time of Jesus.

Saint Luke is the author of two of the longer books of the New Testament—his Gospel and The Acts of the Apostles. In several narrations in The Acts of the Apostles, Luke uses the first person plural, *We*, indicating that he was one of the companions of Saint Paul in his travels (see Acts 16:10–17; 20:5–15; 21:1–18; 27:1—28:16).

Saint Luke was a physician by profession, although he does not leave clear indications of it in his Gospel. Traditionally it has been noted that Saint Luke is the only evangelist to mention the bloody sweat of Jesus in the agony in the Garden of Gethsemani, something that would be of special interest for a physician.

One legend describes Saint Luke as an artist—a painter and a sculptor—to whom several images of the Blessed Virgin were attributed. This attribution took place during the iconoclast heresy when holy images were being destroyed by heretics. Some Christians, in order to save their images, stated that they were true and authentic images because they had been made personally by Saint Luke, who had direct contact with the Virgin Mary. The only true image of Mary that Saint Luke left for us is portrayed in the Magnificat, the song of Mary during her visit to her relative Elizabeth.

52. What is the general structure of the Gospel of Saint Luke?

We should remember that Saint Luke's Gospel is just the first part of his two works that include The Acts of the Apostles. The beginning of each separate book of Saint Luke's writing has a formal and solemn introduction, dedicating his work to Theophilus, who probably was a Christian well known in the community, who had converted from paganism.

Saint Luke had already found a tradition and a general structure for his Gospel in the work of Saint Mark, which he follows freely with some omissions and transpositions, adding and highlighting some themes that Luke considers especially important. For Saint Luke, the entire Gospel is the story of the pilgrimage of Jesus, starting in his native place of Nazareth and ending in Jerusalem and in heaven. After 9:51, Saint Luke speaks repeatedly of Jesus' journey to Jerusalem (see 9:51; 13:22; 17:11), looking toward the passion, resurrection, and ascension of Jesus.

For Saint Luke, the three years of Jesus' ministry on earth are the three most important years in the history of humanity. The Old Testament announced and prepared the coming of Jesus. The entire public life of Jesus, from the first discourse in Nazareth, fulfills the hopes and expectations of the Old Testament as it had been previously predicted in the Canticles of Zechariah and Mary. The Acts of the Apostles continues the teachings of Luke's Gospel and the fulfillment of the promises.

Saint Luke begins his Gospel with a prologue that is followed by the infancy narrative, the preaching of John the Baptist, the genealogy of Jesus starting with Adam, the temptations in the desert, and the great journey from Nazareth to heaven. Along this journey, Saint Luke places many of the teachings that Saint Matthew had placed in the great discourses of Jesus.

53. When and where did Saint Luke write his Gospel?

It is generally believed that Saint Luke wrote his Gospel around the years AD 80 to 85. Saint Luke's Gospel has many details that relate to the Gospel of Saint John, which was written in its final form rather late. It is surprising that Saint Luke makes no reference to the letters of Saint Paul; it is believed that when Saint Luke wrote, the letters of Saint Paul had not been yet compiled. If Saint Luke had access to witnesses of the preaching of Jesus, as well as to Saint Mark and other sources, he could not have written too early or too late.

Some scholars believe that some of the letters attributed to Saint Paul may have been written by Saint Luke, since he well knew the mind and theology of the apostle Paul.

The Gospel of Saint Luke seems to have been produced in the midst of Greek culture, when the Christian Church was being extended within the Roman Empire. It must have been written in an area where there was an important Jewish community; many think that it might have been written in Antioch, where there was a flourishing Christian community. The Christians for whom Saint Luke wrote must have had a considerable knowledge of the Old Testament; they may have been "old Christians."

Certainly, Saint Luke wrote after the destruction of Jerusalem by the Romans, for he alludes to it by providing more concrete details than the other Gospels (see Lk 19:41–44; 21:20–24); as noted, it is believed that Saint Luke wrote about AD 85.

54. What is Luke's impression or concept of Jesus when he writes his Gospel?

Saint Luke seems to think of Jesus on several different levels, depending on the theme of each narrative. In the infancy narratives, Jesus is the incarnated Son of God who comes to bring fulfillment to the promises and hopes of the Old Testament. In some sections, Luke recalls the old prophets of Israel, who call the people to conversion while denouncing the evils that afflicted them. Jesus will walk resolutely toward Jerusalem, the city where the prophets met their fate (see Lk 13:34).

The principal image of Jesus in the third Gospel is that of a pilgrim who brings a message of conversion, forgiveness, and salvation to all he meets along the way. The pilgrimage of the Word will be continued with the mission of Saint Paul in The Acts of the Apostles, from Jerusalem, through Athens, until Rome. The Word moves from the religious center of the world, passes through its cultural center, and finally comes to the political and military center in the west of the Roman Empire.

A very important point in Luke's Gospel is that Jesus fulfills the hopes of the poor. The first words of the adult Jesus, in the discourse of Nazareth are, "Today this scripture has been fulfilled in your hearing" (Lk 4:21). John the Baptist, the last and greatest of the prophets, had rejoiced in his mother's womb when he recognized the presence of Jesus—he already realized that the promises made by the prophets in favor of the poor and the oppressed were going to finally become a reality. The canticles of Zechariah and Mary repeat that God has begun to fulfill what he promised in favor of the poor. Jesus is the fulfiller and the fulfillment of the promises and hopes of the Old Testament.

55. What are the principal themes and teachings of Luke's Gospel?

At the beginning of his Gospel, in the prologue addressed to Theophilus, Saint Luke says that he wants to give assurances and confirmation of the faith of his readers. Saint Luke was seeking to direct the behavior of Christians guided by their faith, while they were living in the Greek and Roman world, where there were enormous differences between the rich and the poor, and where a great majority of the population was composed of servants and slaves.

Saint Luke recalls that salvation began with the promises of God to Israel and with the divine providence and protection of God for the Israelites during Old Testament times. The promises to Israel have now become promises for the Christian community. The decree by Emperor Augustus ordering a census of his subjects was nothing but an instrument in the hands of God so that Jesus would be born in Bethlehem. The Spirit of God guides the activity of Jesus during his ministry and continues to guide the newborn church in Jerusalem.

Saint Luke wrote after the destruction of Jerusalem by the Romans and was convinced that the second coming of Jesus was going to be considerably delayed. Christians had to define their relationship with their surrounding world where materialism, power, and wealth were the guiding rules for the behavior of many. Christians had to live in that world without becoming part of it. Some think that Luke's Gospel, like The Acts of the Apostles, was written to present a positive image of the Christian faith to the Roman authorities because since Nero's reign the Christians could be considered dangerous or suspicious.

The Gospel of Saint Luke contains some of the most beautiful parables of the New Testament, some of which are listed as follows:

- 10:25–37 The Good Samaritan
- 12:13–21 The Rich Fool
- 15:11–32 The Prodigal Son
- 16:19–31 The Rich Man and Lazarus

Through his Gospel and Acts, Saint Luke stresses several themes; the most important are as follows:

1. God has a plan for salvation that embraces all of human history. The genealogy of Jesus starts with Adam.
2. The Holy Spirit guides Jesus and the Church.
3. God is the Lord of mercy, compassion, and forgiveness.
4. The worth and dignity of women.
5. The responsibilities of the rich toward the poor.

56. What sources did Saint Luke use to write his Gospel?

Saint Luke accompanied Saint Paul in several of his travels, so he certainly also had contact with other apostles in his visits to Jerusalem. Luke points out that he had contacts with other preachers of the new faith, some of whom had known Jesus personally. It is improbable that Saint Luke had personal contacts with Mary the mother of Jesus, since she had probably died long before the time of Saint Luke's writing.

Saint Luke used the Gospel of Saint Mark as reference and for inspiration; certain passages coincide verbatim. He also had access to a source named "Q" that contained the sayings and teachings of Jesus. This same source was also used by Saint Matthew as seen in the verbal accounts of the two Gospels. An important source for Saint Luke was the Greek text of the Old Testament (called the Septuagint or the version of the seventy interpreters). Saint Luke knew the text of this Bible well, adopting much of its vocabulary and even imitating its style (as seen in the canticles of Zechariah, Mary, and Simeon).

The discourses of Jesus in Luke's Gospel, and later those of Peter and Paul in The Acts of the Apostles, follow the rules of Greek writers who put on the lips of their characters the discourses that could have been delivered on special occasions and through which the mind of the speaker was disclosed.

It is more probable that the narrative of the infancy of Jesus is his personal creation, inspired by narratives from the Old Testament. The genealogy of Jesus could come from Jewish sources unknown to us.

57. What is Saint Luke's aim in writing about the infancy of Jesus (Lk 1—2)?

Luke writes with great care and artistry in his narrative of the infancy of Jesus. The birth announcements of the two children—John the Baptist and Jesus—are followed by two nativity scenes, all stressing the preeminence of Jesus over John the Baptist. Both announcements are similar to those in the Old Testament. When a child was born to a woman who had been sterile for a long time, the child was seen as a miracle and a gift from God. Jesus, by being born of a virgin, is the greatest gift from God for humanity. As in Matthew's Gospel, the stories of the infancy of Jesus in Luke's Gospel also look toward the future and the mission of Jesus.

For Catholics it is important to remember that the narrations of the infancy of Jesus are meditated in the recitation of the mysteries of the rosary. Those mysteries reveal what Saint Luke had in mind in writing this section of the Gospel. The mysteries deal with the different *comings* of Jesus to people who probably represent groups who were awaiting the coming of the Savior. At a literal, and even fundamentalist level, the stories can be read as if they were simply historical events. At a theological level, the deeper intention of the evangelist can be appreciated by noting that he presents responses of happiness of persons to Jesus' coming into the world. At a pastoral level, we are called to realize that the comings of Jesus continue to be a truth and an experience in the lives of believers of every period of history.

1. *The Annunciation:* The important element is not just the coming of the angel and of the Holy Spirit to Mary. It is the *Incarnation* of the Son of God, who comes to Mary's womb, that fills Mary with Joy.
2. *The Visitation:* It is not just the visit of Mary to Elizabeth but foremost is the visit of Jesus to his cousin, John the Baptist. John is filled with joy even in his mother's womb.

3. *The Birth of Jesus in Bethlehem:* At the first Christmas, the people filled with joy were the shepherds who had received the joyful message from an angel; shepherds were poor and exploited people.

4. *The Presentation of Jesus in the Temple:* Again, this is more than the simple fulfillment of a duty from the Law of Moses. Jesus finally came to Simeon and Anne, who had been waiting for years for the fulfillment of their hope and faith.

5. *The Child Lost in the Temple:* Jesus has come to different types of people, but sooner or later Jesus gets "lost" or people experience the absence of Jesus. The disciples will experience that loss on Good Friday. Believers often will have to wait, possibly in tears, until Jesus makes himself manifest to them again in faith.

58. What is the teaching of the annunciation by the angel to Mary (Lk 1:26–38)?

The narration of the annunciation by the angel who appears to Mary also can be seen as the vocation of Mary. When an annunciation is made in the Scriptures, the recipient usually is asked to have faith and to accept the message as given. Zechariah failed in this respect.

Mary responds to the angel without any hesitance, accepting the role God offers her, although Mary asks how it will take place, since she is a virgin. The day of the annunciation Mary receives three gifts (or three visits): that of the angel, that of the Holy Spirit, and that of Jesus, which is the most important. It is the day of the *Incarnation* of the Son of God.

Jesus comes to live in the midst of his people, in the womb of Mary, to begin a new creation. Luke's narration is an echo of similar annunciations in the Old Testament. In addition to being an individual person, Mary is also the type or model of the poor of the Lord, of those humble and sincere persons who placed all their trust in God and had all their hopes in him.

Mary receives a double message: (1) her son will be Son of the Most High and Son of David; he will reign on the throne of his father David; and (2) her son will be the Holy One, the Son of God.

Mary knows, like Abraham and Sarah (see Gen 18:14), that nothing is impossible for God. With this knowledge she declares herself the humble servant of the Lord, ready to accept his will.

While praying this mystery of the rosary, one may meditate on the humility, faith, and openness of Mary, who received the joyful announcement that the Savior would come to her and in her. The prayers of this mystery can be offered for families or friends who are simple and humble persons of faith, so that Jesus will come now, once again, into them so that they will experience the joy Mary experienced on the day of the annunciation.

59. What special message do we receive from the visit of Mary to her relative Elizabeth (Lk 1:39–56)?

Mary had said that she was the handmaid of the Lord; now she went on to become a handmaid of her relative in need of help because of her advanced age. Mary does not think about herself, her own prestige, or dignity after the announcement of the angel. She hurries to go to her relative who herself has received a gift of God that she had desired for a long time.

In this joyful mystery we may meditate not so much on the encounter and meeting of the two women but in the joy of John the Baptist in recognizing the presence of Jesus. John is the last and the greatest of the prophets who feels that the old promises of God in favor of Israel and of the poor and the humble finally are going to be fulfilled with Jesus.

Mary pronounces her canticle, the Magnificat, written by Saint Luke and inspired in a similar birth song of the Old Testament (see 1 Sam 2:1–10). Mary praises the Lord for the great things he has done in his humble servant and in favor also of the poor and the humble throughout all of history: He humbles the proud and lifts up the lowly, he brings down the mighty from their thrones, and fills the poor in with good things.

While praying this mystery, one may meditate on the prophets of our time—people who are fighting for respect and the dignity of the poor and oppressed. Prayers are needed so that their struggles and efforts will proceed according to the values of the Gospel, so that Jesus will also come to them, bringing them joy, so that they may persevere in their efforts.

60. What special meaning does Saint Luke see in the birth of Jesus in Bethlehem (Lk 2:1–20)?

From the very beginning Saint Luke points out that Emperor Augustus, who considered himself the master of the world, was just a simple person in the hands of God who was bringing about his plans for the future of the world. The Messiah had to be born in Bethlehem, and the decree of the emperor made this possible.

Jesus is born in a poor place, like the poor were usually born, without baby showers or celebrations and even without a crib; a manger suffices for the one who is the King of the Universe, for the one who later will not find a place to rest his head.

The day of Jesus' birth, the people who receive the news with great joy are the poor shepherds. They were exploited persons, despised and discriminated against; they were the poorest of the poor who had to work day and night, without rest. An angel comes to the shepherds to announce to them first the good news of the Gospel. God ignored the powerful and invited the poor and the humble. Herod and the priests did not know that had happened; only the poor knew.

Mary is presented as a theologian who tries to understand—to make sense of—what was taking place. The message of the angel, and now the visit of the shepherds, begin to become pieces of a puzzle that she will try to understand all throughout her life.

When praying this mystery of the rosary, one might think of humble and discriminated persons in our society, asking the Lord Jesus to come into their lives, bringing them the joy he brought to the shepherds on that first Christmas day.

61. What is the message in the presentation of the Child Jesus in the Temple (Lk 2:21–40)?

Saint Luke refers to Jesus by calling him the *firstborn* of Mary, not because Mary would have other children but because the evangelist speaks of the special religious legal duties of the family for a firstborn male child.

Jesus, being the firstborn male child, had to be presented in the Temple as required by the Law of Moses (see Ex 13:2; Lev 12:2–8; Num 18:15–16). In the Temple Jesus appears as a poor child among other poor children. They made for him the offering usual for the poor: two turtledoves.

During the presentation of Jesus, the people who experienced a great joy were Simeon and Anna, two elderly persons who for many years had been awaiting the fulfillment of the promises made to them by the Lord. God never fails to fulfill his promises, but it often seems to us that he comes rather late, although he never fails to come. Simeon and Anna received the Child with great joy and gave witness to him to all those around them. Simeon, in his canticle, announced the universality of salvation arriving with Jesus, who would be a light for all the nations and the glory of his people, Israel. Simeon announces to Mary the trials through which she will learn the deep significance of the Incarnation of Jesus and the way of sacrifice, until a sword will pierce her heart on Calvary.

While praying this joyful mystery, one may think of people who have been waiting for long years for the Lord to respond to their prayers and petitions—these could be for the solution of a problem, for the conversion of a spouse or relative, or for the return of a long-lost son. Some people, like Simeon and Anna, have been waiting for years for an answer to their prayers.

62. What is the special message in the story of the Child Jesus lost in the Temple (Lk 2:41–52)?

When Jesus turned twelve years old, he was considered an adult, and as such he had to observe the prescriptions of the Law of Moses. Three times a year Jews were obligated to go to Jerusalem for the celebration of the three great Jewish feasts, Passover, Pentecost, and Tabernacles or Tents (see Dt 16:1–6). Sometimes, especially during Passover, towns in Galilee were empty because all the inhabitants had gone up to Jerusalem.

Jesus purposely got lost in Jerusalem, staying behind in the Temple. His intent was to announce in some way his future and to teach his own parents a lesson. For three days, Joseph and Mary looked for the lost Jesus in anguish. Later in the Gospels, the disciples, from Good Friday to Easter, will feel the anguish of having lost Jesus. On the third day, Jesus' parents find him in the Temple amidst scribes and doctors of the law. The week before his passion, Jesus goes to the Temple every day and discusses the law with its doctors, who marvel again at the wisdom of his answers (see Lk 21:37–38).

It is worth noticing that in this narration we find the first words that Saint Luke ascribes to Jesus in his Gospel: "Why were you searching for me?" (Lk 2:40). These words are similar to the first words of Jesus in John's Gospel at the beginning of Jesus' public ministry: "What are you looking for?" (Jn1:38). The whole life of Christians is a search. Jesus sets an example, making of his own life a search to do the will of the Father and to give him glory.

Saint Luke says that the parents of Jesus did not understand the answer he gave them, but Jesus still obeyed them and returned home with them to Galilee. This is especially significant for us now, when we find teenagers who complain because their parents do not understand them. We can tell them that they are in good company, since Jesus himself was not understood by his parents but he obeyed them nevertheless.

The Gospel repeats that Mary continued to treasure these memories in her heart, meditating on their meaning. Mary's entire life was a process of faith, trying to understand the personality of her Son, letting him free to carry out his mission. This is a challenge for mothers even in our own time.

63. Why does Saint Luke place so much emphasis on the social dimension of the preaching of John the Baptist (Lk 3:1–18)?

The preaching of John the Baptist was a surprise to the Jews. For several centuries they had been waiting for the coming of a prophet who would offer them solutions to age-old problems and give them directions for life. There were national religious problems to be solved under the direction of a prophet (see 1 Mac 4:46; 14:41). After listening to John the Baptist many people thought he was the expected prophet. Great multitudes went to listen to him and to be baptized by him.

Saint Luke places the preaching of John the Baptist in a political and religious context because it was a great event in the history of humanity. The kingdom of God was making its entrance into the world.

Saint Luke, having in mind readers from the Greek and Roman world where there were many slaves and servants, presents the contents of John's preaching that he considered most relevant to address the great inequalities of that society. John the Baptist is a great prophet who received the Word of God just as it had been received by the Old Testament prophets (see Lk 3:2).

For Saint Luke the preaching of the Baptist, in addition to being an event in the political and religious world, is an event filled with social implications. Saint Luke does not tell us anything about John's food or his garments; he adds the social dimension that had not been included by Saint Matthew. True conversion is manifested through a definite social behavior, with concrete actions that affect daily life. Those who have should share with those who have nothing, even to the point of becoming poor with the poor, just as Jesus did. Saint Luke notes that everyone has to answer the call to conversion; no one should trust in titles or privileges of the past. Conversion must be adapted to the life and profession of each person; in their own way and on their terms, each individual will have to take sides with the poor and share with them whenever possible. Saint Luke stresses these points throughout his Gospel.

64. What is special in Saint Luke's narration of the temptations of Jesus (Lk 4:1–13)?

It is important here to recall what was said about the temptations of Jesus in Matthew's Gospel. Jesus was brought into the desert to be tempted— just like the people of Israel in Exodus.

Saint Luke places the genealogy of Jesus before his baptism and the temptations, because Jesus is the representative of all humanity as a people of God, in line with the universalism he proclaims throughout the Gospel. The temptations of Jesus were temptations common to any person in the Greek and Roman world; they are also temptations that people today can have. It was important to stress that the life of the Christian had to be directed by the laws and desires of God and not by his or her own likes and desires.

Saint Luke saw two worlds in conflict: the one of the values of the power of the Roman Empire and the one of the values of Christ. The values of the empire were the seductions of pleasure, power, honors, and riches. In the kingdom of Christ the values are service to the poor and obedience to God.

Saint Luke changed the order of the temptations in the Gospel of Saint Matthew; for Saint Luke, everything important culminates in Jerusalem, as does the third temptation. The central temptation receives special treatment: Saint Luke uses 28 words to describe what Saint Matthew narrated with just eight words (in Greek). The contrast between the two readings is shown on the next page.

Mt 4:8–10	**Lk 4:5–8**
Again, the devil took him to a very high mountain and showed him all the kingdoms of the world and their splendor; and he said to him, "All these I will give you, if you will fall down and worship me."	Then the devil led him up and showed him in an instant all the kingdom of the world. And the devil said to him, "To you I will give their glory and all this authority; for it has been given over to me, and I give it to anyone I please. If you, then, will worship me, it will all be yours."
Jesus said to him,	Jesus answered him,
"Away with you, Satan! for it is written,	"It is written,
'Worship the Lord your God, and serve only him.'"	'Worship the Lord your God, and serve only him.'"

Saint Luke suggests that the devil showed Jesus all the kingdoms of the Roman Empire (*oikumene;* the then-known inhabited areas of the whole earth). This recalls how Moses saw all the Holy Land before he died on Mount Nebo. Saint Luke emphasizes the word *power,* because in the opinion of the evangelist the power and the wealth of the Roman Empire were diabolical, administered by the devil; the empire had persecuted the church and killed the two apostles, Peter and Paul. It is not surprising that Luke thinks in terms of the empire being at war with the church. Christians had to decide whether they were going to accept the values and the way of life governed by power and wealth or whether they were going to renounce those values in their lifestyle.

65. What is the special meaning of the discourse of Jesus in the synagogue of Nazareth (Lk 4:14–30)?

The inaugural discourse of Jesus in his home at Nazareth contains the first words of the adult Jesus at the beginning of his public ministry: "Today this Scripture has been fulfilled in your hearing." For Saint Luke, the fulfillment of the prophecies and hopes of the Old Testament are basic—as emphasized in the infancy narratives and in the canticles of Zechariah and of Mary (see Lk 1:55, 70). Jesus is bringing the final fulfillment.

This discourse marks the beginning of Jesus' public ministry and announces some of the values that will guide his actions. In this Gospel, Jesus does not visit the same town or place twice; his ministry is a pilgrimage that starts in Nazareth and ends in Jerusalem. The disciples will continue the pilgrimage of the Word and go forth until the ends of the world. Saint Luke offers a solemn presentation of the message of Jesus, quoting the prophet Isaiah (see Is 61:1–2). We have here the Jesus who will be presented in the Gospel: one who receives and accepts all kinds of poor and needy people: sick, oppressed, discriminated, rejected, criminals, aliens, sinners, women, and even prostitutes. Everyone finds a place in the heart of Jesus.

Jesus explains how in the Old Testament the poor and discriminated had been the object of God's preferences: the widow of Sarepta as told by the prophet Elijah in 1 Kings 17:8–24 (in Lk 7:11–17 this is the widow of Naim), and the Syrian leper Naaman healed by the prophet Elisha in 2 Kings 5:1–14 (in Lk 17:11–19 there are ten lepers who are healed, with only a single grateful one, a despised Samaritan).

Those who heard Jesus' first speech reacted with anger and violence; they did not want this kind of messiah. They wanted one who would bring them power, honors, and wealth. Jesus went through their midst and left them behind. Other persons, open to his message, would be invited by Jesus to follow him and become pilgrims with him.

66. What is the significance of the vocation of the first disciples in Luke's Gospel (Lk 5:1–11)?

Saint Luke places the miraculous catch of fish and the vocation of the disciples at the beginning of the public ministry of Jesus, after the discourse of Nazareth. Saint John narrates this miracle in the last chapter of his book.

The miraculous catch of fish is filled with symbolism for Saint Luke; it presents a model for working in the Christian community. In the church, the new boat of Peter, Jesus makes Peter the leader of the group. Jesus gives Peter the directions that everyone must follow. The other disciples follow Peter's lead.

Usually, fishing was done at night, when the fish could not see the nets. When the disciples work without Jesus, the work is fruitless. When they work following Jesus' directions, the results are most impressive.

THE GOSPEL OF SAINT LUKE · 75

The evangelist points out that after the miracle, Peter and his companions "…got up, left everything, and followed him" (Lk 5:28). According to Saint Luke, one cannot be an authentic fisher of men without a spirit of poverty and evangelical detachment from ties to material things.

According to the spirit of this narration, we Catholics see in the successor of Peter, in the pope, the chosen person who continues to direct the boat of Peter, the Catholic Church. He has received a mission from Jesus and has his grace. We all work under his guidance, according to the desires of Jesus.

67. What are the similarities between the Sermon on the Plain (by Saint Luke) and the Sermon on the Mount (by Saint Matthew) (Lk 6:17–49)?

The discourses of Jesus in the Gospels of Saints Matthew and Luke have a similar content, although Saint Luke has omitted the questions related to the observance of the Law of Moses that are so important in Saint Matthew's text. Greek readers were not so keen on the importance of the Law of Moses. Much of the teaching in Matthew's Sermon on the Mount had been placed by Luke along Jesus' journey from Galilee to Jerusalem.

While Matthew locates Jesus' sermon on a mountain (since a mountain had been a place for the revelation of God to Moses), Luke speaks of a plain, recalling the expanse of the desert where God had fed his hungry people during the Exodus. For Saint Luke, the mountain is the place where Jesus goes for prayer, much more than a place for revelation.

The two discourses begin with the Beatitudes. In Luke's Gospel the Beatitudes are followed by curses that prepare the context for the rest of the discourse (see Lk 6:20–26). The evangelist contrasts the virtues of the disciples (see Lk 6:20–23) and the lifestyle of the rich and the powerful of his time (see Lk 6:24–26). Saint Luke also takes aim at the false prophets who preached comfort in life and did not really call people to conversion and sacrifice (see Lk 6:26). It is possible that some in Luke's community were inclined to the lifestyle of the rich.

Jesus' demands in Luke's Gospel are much more radical than those found in Matthew's Gospel, especially in reference to detachment from material things. The center of the discourse is found in verses 6:27–38, and the text preceding and following this section is just the framework. Saint Matthew speaks of the love of enemies, of those who persecute us (see Mt

5:44); for Saint Luke, enemies are those who hate, curse, and abuse us (see Lk 6:27–28). Saint Matthew asks for generosity for the one who begs from us (see Mt 5:42); Saint Luke speaks of the one who robs you and whom you must not go after (see Lk 6:30). In Luke's Gospel, the golden rule of doing to others what you wish others to do unto you, has a context of generosity and detachment from material wealth. This detachment is emphasized in Luke 6:34–35, a detail not found in Matthew's text:

If you lend to those from whom you hope to receive, what credit is that to you? Even sinners lend to sinners, to receive as much again. But love your enemies, do good, and lend, expecting nothing in return. Your reward will be great, and you will be children of the Most High; for he is kind to the ungrateful and the wicked.

Saint Luke's sermon concludes, as in Saint Matthew's version, with a call to practice what Jesus says, especially in the context of generosity and detachment from material wealth.

68. How does Saint Luke present women in his Gospel?

Saint Luke tells us that in addition to the twelve apostles, a group of women were followers of Jesus. Even now some find it difficult to envision this. Thanks to this group of women, the apostles could pay more attention to their ministry, since the women "...provided for them out of their resources" (Lk 8:3).

Chapters 7 to 10 of Luke's Gospel contain several narratives referring to women:

7:11–17	The widow of Nain and the compassion of Jesus
7:36–50	The anointing of Jesus by a woman sinner
8:1–3	The women who accompanied Jesus
10:38–42	The hospitality of Martha and Mary

Saint Luke names some of the women, saying later that they had followed Jesus all the way from Galilee (see Lk 23:27). Those women were just as much followers of Jesus as the twelve disciples. Possibly these are the same women in The Acts of the Apostles who are gathered in prayer with the apostles and also receive with them the Holy Spirit on Pentecost (see Acts 1:14).

Among the women who followed Jesus, special attention is given to Mary Magdalene, about whom there has been much publicity in recent times. The mention in the Bible that seven evil spirits had come out of her may be a reference to the fact that she had been a very sickly person who had been healed by Jesus, since sickness was associated with the devil. Readers should not "read into" those words a reference to her moral conduct.

Later, Luke presents another two women, Martha and Mary (see Lk 10:38–42), who are two examples of responses to Jesus: One is all active in serving him food, while the other offers him her ears and her heart.

69. Who was the sinful woman who washed the feet of Jesus in Luke 7:36–50?

The anointing of Jesus by a woman in the Gospels by Mark and John announces and prepares for the passion and resurrection of Jesus (Mk 14:3–7; Jn 12:1–8). In these two Gospels, the objection against the action of the woman because of the waste of something very precious that could have been given to the poor comes from Judas. Everyone is familiar with Jesus' answer to that objection.

Saint Luke praises the actions of the woman sinner and contrasts them with those of the proud and heartless Pharisee who had invited Jesus into his home. The woman was a much better person than the Pharisee. The love and generosity of the woman were more valuable in the eyes of Jesus than the invitation of the Pharisee.

Because of the proximity of this story to that of the women who followed Jesus and served him, since the end of the sixth century this sinful woman has been identified with Mary Magdalene, without solid reasons. For centuries, artists loved to paint Mary Magdalene, half-naked, as a sinner; they also love to paint Saint Sebastian, also half-naked, being shot with arrows by the Roman soldiers. Those were opportunities for their art to paint the human body in an attractive and innocent way.

70. What is the significance of the Great Journey of Jesus from Galilee to Jerusalem in Saint Luke's Gospel (Lk 9:51—19:28)?

Although Saint Luke says that "when the days drew near for him [Jesus] to be taken up, he set his face to go to Jerusalem" (9:51), readers must remember that the entire Gospel is a pilgrimage by Jesus that began in Nazareth. Later Saint Luke repeats that Jesus was "on [the] way" (10:38), that "Jesus went through one town and village after another, teaching as he made his way to Jerusalem" (13:22), and that "large crowds were traveling with him" (14:25). Jesus will remind the disciples that the ascent to Jerusalem has as its goal the fulfillment of the prophecies (see Lk 18:31).

It is fitting to note the importance that Saint Luke ascribes to Jesus' ascent to Jerusalem, keeping in mind his forthcoming passion, death, and resurrection. Jesus is on a mission. For saint Luke, everything that is important in the history of salvation must culminate in Jerusalem, just as we saw happen with the infancy narrative and the temptations of Jesus. The passion, resurrection, and ascension will also happen in the Holy City. After his resurrection Jesus will not go to Galilee ahead of his disciples as in the other Gospels. In Saint Luke's Gospel, Jesus' appearances after his death all happen in Jerusalem and its vicinity.

71. Why does Saint Luke criticize the attachment to material things so harshly (Lk 12:13–21)?

For Saint Luke, attachment to material wealth is foolish and crazy. Jesus asks his own to aim higher and farther than earthly riches. The parable of the Rich Fool suffices in its eloquence. Individuals should not accumulate wealth for themselves but for God. What makes people important is not the wealth that they acquire but the kind of people they are.

The foolish man—rich and prudent in the eyes of the world—in preparing for what is supposed to be a future, forgets that there is a real and more important future that will bring us to an encounter with God, to whom everyone must render an account. The rich fool seems to have forgotten that everything in this world has an end and that God is behind everything. He did not become rich for God.

Later, Saint Luke shows how people can become rich for God: selling what they have and giving alms to the poor. This prepares a treasure in heaven that cannot be lost. Saint Luke also shows us this in the story of Zacchaeus, a rich man, who became truly rich in the eyes of God when he gave half of his goods to the poor.

72. What are the classic parables in Luke's Gospel?

Eight parables play an important role in the theology of Saint Luke. The first are the parables of mercy (see Lk 15:1–32), especially the parable of the Prodigal Son, which proclaims God's infinite mercy.

THE GOSPEL OF SAINT LUKE · 79

The parable of the Good Samaritan (see Lk 10:25–37) teaches that a great and charitable heart knows no racial or religious barriers. We have talked about the parable of the Rich Fool, who was centered in life here and now and forgot to look beyond (see Lk 12:16–21). Saint Matthew spoke about not piling up treasures on earth (see Mt 6:19-21), but Saint Luke speaks of selling and giving alms so as to have a treasure in heaven (see Lk 12:33–34).

The parable of the Unjust Steward (see Lk 16:1–8) invites us to prepare for an eternal future. Every Christian is an administrator of the goods God has entrusted to him or her. We all must "produce fruits" for God. Saint Luke points out that the Pharisees were lovers of money, and they laughed at the teachings of Jesus (see Lk 16:14). In the parable of the Rich Man and Lazarus (see Lk 16:19–31), Jesus announces what will happen to those who heard the law and the prophets every Sabbath in the synagogue (see Lk 16:31). The rich man had ignored the poor man in this life. The poor man Lazarus will find himself in a new world where there will be a radical change in his situation. We are not told that the poor man was a pious person, and the rich man was not a person without some kind of piety; on the contrary, Abraham calls him "son"—to state this more simply, one was poor and the other was rich; one was careless and forgetful of the conditions of the needy person.

The parable of the Pharisee and the Publican (Tax Collector; see Lk 18:9–14) reveals that God's judgments are very different from human judgments and opinions. Those who think of themselves as good persons sometimes are not; besides, people should not compare themselves with others, especially to affirm their own pride and self-love. The world is not divided between good and bad people. In the eyes of God, we are all sinners. Only a few accept that reality; most people deny it.

In the parable of the Wedding Banquet (see Lk 14:15–24; Mt 22:1–14), those invited to the banquet in the Matthew's Gospel give general excuses for not attending. Luke enumerates their excuses by saying that one had bought a field, another five yokes of oxen, and another had just gotten married. Saint Luke underscores the reasons for disregarding the invitation: they were too busy with business and wealth; these things were an obstacle for those who wanted to be good Christians according to the criteria of the evangelist. Saint Luke adds that the refusal of some (in Matthew's Gospel, the Jews; in Luke's, the rich) was the occasion for the invitation to be directed to the poor and the rejected, to those who were usually forgotten.

73. What will the second coming of Jesus, and of the kingdom of God, be like at the end of the world (Lk 17:20–27)?

Saint Luke knew the eschatology of Saint Paul and of Saint Mark, which pointed toward an approaching end of their world and a second coming of the Lord. Jesus had not returned either seven or forty years after his ascension. It was time to rethink and reinterpret the traditional views. The end seemed to be far away. It was necessary to think of the presence of Jesus in the midst of the history of the world as it was unfolding.

Saint Matthew's Gospel contains material similar to that of Saint Luke (see Mt 24:1–44), but Luke adds and sharpens details to give his own personal interpretation. In Luke 14:25—16:31, he provides stern warnings about the use of material wealth. Deep faith was needed to accept his views; thus, the disciples asked Jesus for an increase in their faith (see Lk 17:5). This faith requires much humility (see Lk 17:7-10). Authentic faith will become the source of salvation for people, just as it was for the Samaritan leper, one of the ten healed by Jesus (see Lk 17:11–19). This miracle took place as they were on the way to Jerusalem (see Lk 17:11), where the Jews and the disciples expected the coming of God's kingdom to take place.

Jesus' discourse begins by answering a question from the Pharisees, but the answer is directed toward the disciples. The kingdom of God comes quietly, says Luke (17:20), silently, and is already in the midst of the disciples. The presence of Jesus with them is already the presence of the kingdom of God. Saint Luke presupposes the faith of Christians in this historical presence of the risen Jesus, although Jesus is now visible only to the eyes of faith.

Christian life in the world is a life of faith, although most of us would enjoy seeing the visible glory of Jesus in the world. People eat, drink, buy, sell, plant, build, and marry and are absorbed in the chores of daily life. A believing Christian must not let himself or herself be absorbed by those activities, especially those related to money. Life in the world will follow its routine: "it will be like that on the day that the Son of Man is revealed" (Lk 17:30). Jesus is already in our world, in the Church, but he cannot be seen except by eyes guided by faith. One day God will remove the veil of all nations so that they will see that Jesus was the only savior and hope. That will be a decisive day, a day of judgment and of separations (see Lk 17:31). The Son of Man will not be welcomed with our possessions but with our love and faith.

74. Is it true that Saint Luke condemns the rich (Lk 18:18–30)?

The story of the rich "young" man recalls similar stories in Matthew (see 19:16–22) and Mark (10:17–27). It seems he was not a *young* man since he had fulfilled the commandments since his youth. Saint Luke speaks not of a young man but of one of the rulers [leaders] of the Jews—a rich, influential, and powerful man. For Saint Luke, such a person is the opposite of the poor and of those who are like children and count for little (see Lk 18:15–17).

In Saint Mark's Gospel, Jesus looked at the young man with love (see Mk 10:21). Saint Luke does not show much love for the rich. Jesus asks this rich man to sell everything he has and to give to the poor; then Luke points out that the man was *very* sad because he was *very* rich. Saint Mark says that he went away sad because he had many possessions.

Jesus' warnings in Luke's Gospel are directed to the rich man; others, not the disciples, commented on how difficult it is to be saved. The disciples had been examples of the detachment Jesus was asking from the rich and from anyone who wished to become his disciple. Saint Luke adds that the disciples had left their wives; unlike Saint Mark, he does not say that the disciples will receive possessions in this life. Possessions could constitute a danger, and an obstacle, for the kingdom of God. In The Acts of the Apostles, the Christians of Jerusalem will renounce their possessions and share everything.

75. Why is the story of Zacchaeus so attractive (Lk 19:1–10)?

Zacchaeus is not like the rich man who could not renounce his wealth to follow Jesus (see Lk 18:18–23). He is almost like the disciples described by Luke in 18:28–39. They are rich people who are saved because God makes a miracle in their hearts. Zacchaeus is the friendly rich man who climbs a tree to see Jesus and later shares everything despite the criticism that surrounded him. Zacchaeus is a very popular figure in some biblical circles.

Saint Luke, as it usually happens, tells us much more than what is apparent at first sight. Looking at the context of the narrative, at the story before and at the parable that follows, we can better appreciate the mind of the writer.

The story preceding Zacchaeus tells of the healing of the blind man of Jericho (see Lk 18:35–43). The blind man, like also Zacchaeus, wanted to see, and Jesus opened his eyes. When Jesus opened the eyes of Zacchaeus, he saw himself as rich and thought of the poor; he also saw the possibility that his wealth could have been unjustly won, the fruit of fraud.

The parable after the story of Zacchaeus presents examples of administration of the goods a master had entrusted to his servants. God expects returns from the goods he has entrusted to us. Fruits are produced through generosity toward the poor, just as Zacchaeus had given the example.

Saint Luke enriches his account with many interesting details. The meeting of Jesus and Zacchaeus seems somewhat accidental, since Jesus was just passing by the city; but in God's plans nothing is accidental. Jesus *had* to meet Zacchaeus. This rich man seems to forget his own status and dignity by climbing a tree to see Jesus, just as any poor person might have done. Zacchaeus wanted to see Jesus but when Jesus arrived, it was Jesus who saw Zacchaeus and called him by name. Zacchaeus was overjoyed. As usually happened, the people criticized the behavior of Jesus and made grumbling comments, but neither Jesus nor Zacchaeus seemed to mind them. At some point—probably during the meal—Zacchaeus asked himself why he had received the privilege of Jesus' visit and responded with his generous announcement that he was sharing with the poor. Jesus approved of him and declared him to be a son of Abraham, against all the criticism; he had received the salvation Jesus was offering him.

76. What is special in the Last Supper discourse by Jesus in Luke's Gospel (Lk 22:21–38)?

Saint Luke seems to think of Jesus' farewell supper as if it were some type of Greek banquet, which was usually followed by a dialogue. This dialogue becomes a farewell by Jesus, somewhat similar to the discourse of Saint Paul in The Acts of the Apostles (see Acts 20:18–35). He offers the last will and testament of Jesus. During his account of the Last Supper, Luke does not speak of the treason of Judas; he mentions it later. The other synoptic Gospels tell of the supper without a discourse. Saint John offers the long discourse of Jesus in the Last Supper (see Jn 13—17).

In Saint Luke's Gospel, Jesus is at table with his disciples. In Saint Mark's Gospel, Jesus is with the Twelve. For Saint Luke, Judas, although present, is no longer one of the Twelve. In Saint Mark's Gospel, during the meal, the institution of the Eucharist is a liturgical rite rather than a meal. The eleven disciples are the faithful ones who have not betrayed their Lord. It was very important for Jesus to have a last meal with them. He had to reveal to them his deepest desires for the future and for the church, where his own will continue celebrating this meal, sharing his Body and his Blood. The Eucharist will be the center of the church and of the community. The disciples drink from the same cup as Jesus, implying their identification with him in his passion and the fact that they are his intimate friends. To drink from the cup of a king was a great privilege and a sign of intimacy with him.

The leaders of the church must remember that they receive Jesus in the Eucharist to become like him. Judas is alluded to, without being named, to say that he was not one of the group. Judas, since Luke 22:3–6, has sold himself to money, a terrible crime from the perspective of Saint Luke. The disciples do not ask Jesus about the identity of the traitor; they ask each other, almost as if they could not believe that someone would be capable of betraying the Teacher.

Jesus reminds them that leadership in the church, in the Eucharist, is one of humble service. Jesus has given his own personal example. The greater ones, the elders, must be like the youngest who render the most humble and lowly services to the others; leaders are called to be servants. Jesus' entire ministry has been an example of service to the poor, sinners, criminals, and marginalized. Leaders in the church must follow in the footsteps of Jesus, avoiding the ambitions of the rich and the powerful.

Jesus' recommendation to his disciples about arming themselves has been discussed at length; they had two swords, but the disciples did not seem to understand Jesus' meaning. In the Garden of Gethsemani, Jesus rejects the recourse to arms. Did Jesus approve the behavior of the good thief who had been a guerrilla fighter? The good thief had fought against the Romans for the freedom of his people. He heard the promise of Jesus that on that very day he would be in paradise with him; he would be really free. Jesus was not speaking of the material swords that the disciples already possessed. He wanted for them something stronger and from within: faith and detachment from material wealth; that would be their strength. But when Saint Luke wrote his Gospel for the Christians of the Roman Empire, after the uprising of the Jews against the Romans, some Christians could consider as criminals those of their brothers who had fought and suffered fighting the Romans. Roman Christians wanted to be patriotic, but they were not to condemn those who participated in the struggle against Rome. If they were criminals, they were like the good thief, and they were dying like Jesus.

77. What are the most important points of the narration of the passion by Saint Luke?

Saint Luke, like the other Gospel writers, stresses that Jesus dies as innocent and just, like a lamb sacrificed for the salvation of his people. Jesus is also the prophet who must die in Jerusalem, like the prophets of old.

Jesus is a model in forgiving; he gives an example to his own of what he had been preaching. The compassion of Jesus toward others in the midst of his own sufferings is remarkable:

1. Jesus consoles the women of Jerusalem who lament over him.
2. The first word of Jesus in the cross is one of forgiveness for his enemies.
3. Jesus announces forgiveness and salvation to the converted thief.
4. Jesus dies with full confidence in his Father.

Saint Luke does not quote Psalm 22:1 regarding the feeling of abandonment of Jesus on the cross, because Jesus, in life and in death, is never alone. Saint Luke quotes Psalm 31:5, "into your hand I commit my spirit." This psalm was recited by Jews in their evening prayer and expresses the certainty of resurrection and new life. Before his final sleep, Jesus entrusts himself not to the Lord but to the Father, full of trust in him. Saint Stephen, the first martyr, will follow the example of Jesus in his death with words of forgiveness for his enemies (see Acts 7:60) and entrusting his spirit to the hands of Jesus (see Acts 7:59).

Jesus dies along with a criminal who accompanies him to paradise. Saint Luke repeatedly affirms Jesus' innocence. The Roman centurion at the foot of the cross recognizes that Jesus is a just and innocent man, not a criminal. In The Acts of the Apostles, Saint Luke repeats that Jesus was the *Righteous One* (see Acts 3:14; 7:55; 22:14). Jesus was treated like a criminal; it is possible that Saint Luke could be thinking of some Christians who were treated as criminals, because they had joined the rebellion against the Romans and suffered the same fate as Jesus.

It is possible that in declaring Jesus just (righteous) and innocent, Saint Luke is also thinking of Isaiah 53:11 and Wisdom 2:18 and 3:2–4. The just man is one who is not appreciated and is rejected and despised by the rich and the powerful; the just man is one who places all his trust in the Lord and not in the powers of the world. Such was Jesus in life and death in the Gospel of Saint Luke.

78. What lessons are taught in the story of the disciples going to Emmaus (Lk 24:13–5)?

The last thing Jesus does in Saint Luke's Gospel is accompany the disciples on a journey. Jesus meets them, walks with them, and teaches them in order to open their minds to see the hand of God in what they considered a great tragedy in their life. The goal of this journey is to bring the disciples back to faith and hope and to prepare the last apparition to the apostles. Professional catechists have seen in this narration a model for teaching about the Christian faith:

- Jesus approaches the disciples; he has a plan and a message.
- Jesus likes to hear from their own lips how they perceive the situation, although he knows it well.
- The disciples open their hearts to Jesus.
- The disciples had been so downcast that they could not believe the good news, especially since women were the messengers.
- Jesus reproaches them; they are hard at heart, rather than hard of mind.
- Jesus opens their mind and explains to them God's plan in accordance with the Scriptures.
- Jesus appears to go farther…into the night.
- Jesus desired to be invited.
- In the breaking of the bread, in the Eucharist, they recognized him. Did they have a memory from the Last Supper? The Christians in Saint Luke's Gospel recognized the presence of Jesus in their eucharistic celebrations.
- The disciples went back to the community they had left.

- The disciples gave witness of their experience of Jesus and of how they had recognized him.
- They listened to the witness of the other apostles who already believed.
- They saw Jesus, once again, in the midst of the community.

Why did the disciples not recognize Jesus before, while their hearts were burning at the hearing of the Scriptures? In Luke's community the sharing of the Scriptures was the preparation for the breaking of the bread and for the experience of the new presence of Jesus in the community. It is interesting that there are two meals in the Bible after which the eyes of those eating are opened. The first is that of Adam and Eve, whose eyes were opened after eating the forbidden fruit and seeing themselves naked. In the first meal of the risen Jesus—the new Adam—the eyes of the disciples are opened to recognize his presence.

79. When and how did the ascension of Jesus take place? Where is Jesus now?

In his Gospel, Saint Luke places the ascension of Jesus on Easter Sunday, after the only apparition of Jesus to the apostles. In The Acts of the Apostles, the ascension takes place forty days *after* the resurrection. It is useless to ask fundamentalists "When did it really happen?" Saint Luke's writings are theological and catechetical in nature and aim. We must ask what Saint Luke was trying to communicate through each one of those narrations.

The narration of the ascension in the Gospel usually serves as a final touch to the ministry of Jesus on earth. In The Acts of the Apostles the ascension narrative introduces and opens the activity of the church on earth, guided by the Holy Spirit.

In the Acts narration of the ascension, another coming of Jesus is promised; many think of it as the Second Coming. For Saint Luke this new coming happens when the Spirit of Jesus descends on the apostles so that they may assume Jesus' ministry and mission. The Acts version reminds us of the prophet Elijah's ascension in a fiery chariot. His disciple, the prophet Elisha, inherited the powers and mission of his teacher because he saw him taken up to heaven. Luke repeats that the disciples saw Jesus going up and that they would be clothed with the Spirit from above to receive the powers of Jesus and continue his mission.

The Jesus who ascended into heaven is now found in the heart of each believer, for we can say with Saint Paul that "it is no longer I who live, but it is Christ who lives in me" (Gal 2:20).

80. How is the Gospel of Saint Luke related to The Acts of the Apostles?

The Gospel of Saint Luke flows into The Acts of the Apostles; it is the second half of the work of Saint Luke. In Acts, the teachings of the Gospel are continued and confirmed. Jesus' physical departure did not constitute an end; it became a new beginning and a new stage in the history of salvation. Some of the common points in both books include the following:

- The salvation of all nations announced in the Luke's Gospel becomes a reality in The Acts of the Apostles when the Christian message reaches to the end of the earth.
- The promises of the Gospel are *fulfilled* in Acts.
- As in Luke's Gospel, The Acts of the Apostles begins with prayer and the action of the Holy Spirit in the midst of a joyful community.
- The poor of the Gospel are exemplified in the first community of Jerusalem.
- Jesus' activity continues through the miracles of the apostles.
- The thousands present for the multiplication of the bread correspond to the thousands who are converted on the day of Pentecost.
- Saint Paul, like Jesus in his passion, must appear before governors and kings.
- Jesus and his message are very alive in the newborn church.
- Just as Luke's Gospel had been a fulfillment of prophecies and hopes, so too is The Acts of the Apostles.
- The opposition of the Jews to the message of Jesus is carried along in both of Saint Luke's works.
- Throughout Luke's work he makes an effort to justify Jesus and Saint Paul and to diminish the responsibility of Roman authorities.
- It is surprising that Saint Luke does not speak directly about the destruction of Jerusalem and the Temple, which had already happened. Perhaps the mention of these events would have been like shaking a wasp nest in the face of the Roman Empire.

5

THE GOSPEL
OF SAINT JOHN

81. Who is the author of the fourth Gospel?

As noted previously, in ancient times the concept of *author* was not the same as ours now. An author could be a person who had directly written a work; it could be also the person who had dictated the work or inspired the ideas of the book (as could have happened with some of the Letters of Saint Paul) or just someone from whom the ideas or doctrines of the work, whether directly or indirectly, are derived.

Generally it is believed that the *spiritual author* of the fourth Gospel was the apostle John, although the material author could have been a secretary or one of his disciples who transmitted or interpreted the ideas and teachings of the apostle. Some authors speak of a redactor or a compiler who completed the work originated from the apostle and gave it the current form it has in the Bible.

Since the time of Saint Irenaeus, bishop of Lyons (c. AD 180), the fourth Gospel has been attributed to Saint John, the son of Zebedee, who would also be the beloved disciple. Saint Irenaeus wanted to associate the origins of this Gospel with Jesus and the apostles to deny the claims of Gnostic heretics of his time. According to church historian Eusebius, Saint Irenaeus received his information from Saint Polycarp, bishop of Smyrna (d. AD 156), who had been a disciple of Saint John the evangelist.

The attribution of this Gospel to John the apostle seems to be suggested by the fact that the Gospel provides more proper names of disciples than any other Gospel, never mentioning the two sons of Zebedee, James and John, although these two brothers are close to Jesus in the other three Gospels. Some scholars believe that the evangelist, out of humility, did not include himself or his brother in the narration; there may be some truth to this approach, but these two brothers must have suffered an early martyrdom and death, long before the Gospels were written. The prediction by Jesus of the death of the two disciples, drinking from the same chalice as Jesus and being baptized with the same baptism (see Mk 10:39), probably had been fulfilled by the time Mark wrote his Gospel. Saint James, according to The Acts of the Apostles, was the first disciple to be martyred (see Acts 12:2).

As noted in the introduction to the Gospels, the author of John's Gospel is probably the author of the three letters attributed to the apostle. The author of the Book of Revelation is a different person, although his work has some verbal and theological points that are similar to John's Gospel.

The author of the fourth Gospel is a Jew who writes for a mixed community of Christians coming from Judaism and paganism. The last chapter of John (chapter 21) attributes the Gospel to the beloved disciple without naming him. This disciple could have written or inspired the work. But the last chapter was added to the gospel as an epilogue (c. AD 90 or later) to explain why that disciple had died and to affirm the role of Peter in the Christian community.

82. When and where was John's Gospel written?

Traditionally it has been believed that Saint John's was the last Gospel written, toward the end of the first century, although some opinions offer a much earlier date—about the time that Saint Mark's Gospel was written (AD 70).

Some passages in the Gospel indicate that the city of Jerusalem had not yet been destroyed by the Romans (see Jn 5:2); other passages reflect on the conflicts of the Christian community with Jewish authorities (c. AD 90), when Christians were being excluded from the synagogue. However, The Acts of the Apostles and the Letters of Saint Paul show that the conflicts of the new church with the synagogue started rather early.

John's Gospel has two conclusions (at the end of the last two chapters, Jn 20:30–33 and 21:24–25). There are also two summaries of the public ministry of Jesus with explanations about the incredulity of the Jews (see 12:34–36 and 12:37–50). Many authors have written about the apparent disorder of the narratives and Jesus' discourses of Jesus, which might prompt the opinion that Saint John's Gospel was written in two stages:

one relatively early and another sometime later around the two dates previously mentioned.

In the second stage of writing, in the final and present form of the Gospel, the original text was complemented with additional narrations and teaching that responded to the new challenges facing the community. In this final form, the Gospel was reordered so that now some chapters do not connect well with each other (see chapters 4 to 6), because these sections correspond to stories and sections that appear in the second part of the Gospel.

It is generally accepted that John's Gospel was written during the Jewish *diaspora,* in the region of Ephesus in Asia Minor (today's Turkey); this is the area of the seven churches of the Book of Revelation (see Rev 2—9). In Asia Minor there was severe conflict between the new faith and Judaism and Greek paganism (see Rev 2:9, 13). We have insufficient evidence to reject this traditional opinion.

83. Who was "the beloved disciple," and how is he connected with the Gospel of Saint John?

Since the time of Saint Irenaeus the apostle John, the son of Zebedee, has been considered the disciple for whom Jesus had a special love. Today, many biblical scholars find it difficult to accept this opinion. Some consider "the beloved disciple" to be a symbolic and ideal figure who represents all the disciples of Jesus whom he loved and to whom he entrusted his mother at the foot of the cross. The role of Christians would be to accept and receive the mother of Jesus just as the disciple did.

Still others think that the title of "beloved disciple" is a proud title that lacks modesty or humility; because of this they think that the beloved disciple is not a real physical person but just a symbol. Others see in this title a way of honoring the apostle by the redactor of the Gospel by using words to describe him that are intended to reflect admiration and respect.

It is important to notice that John's Gospel speaks of two mysterious figures: One is "the other disciple" or "another" who appears from the beginning of the Gospel up to the passion (see 18:15; 20:2, 3, 4, 8); the other "is the disciple whom Jesus loved," who is mentioned at the Last Supper and in the passion (Jn 13:23; 19:26; 21:7, 20). Many consider both titles to refer to one and the same person, although it cannot be proven to be so. If the beloved disciple was one of the twelve apostles, he would have been present at the Last Supper, at the foot of the cross, and later would have gone to the sepulcher with Saint Peter. It would have to be the apostle John, who in The Acts of the Apostles is presented in close association with Saint Peter.

Throughout the centuries, the Fathers of the Church and commentators on the Gospel have provided their opinions on the identity of the beloved disciple. In addition to the apostle John, some have thought of Saint Matthias, Saint Mark, Lazarus, Mary Magdalene (especially in the past few years), and Nathanael (from Cana in Galilee, who on the day of his wedding, after the miracle of Jesus, left his wife to become a disciple; because of this he would have been specially loved by Jesus).

Gospel texts suggest that the believed disciple could well be Lazarus, the brother of Martha and Mary. We are told that Lazarus was the one Jesus loved (see Jn 11:3), and that people commented on how much Jesus loved him (see Jn 11:36). We do not know the origin of his friendship with Jesus; they might have known each other from the days of the preaching of John the Baptist (see Jn 1:35). People may have believed that Lazarus was never going to die (see Jn 21:23), since he had already died once and so would have been expected to be alive until the second coming of Jesus. Some have noted that Jesus had been present near the tomb of Lazarus and later Lazarus had been present near the tomb of Jesus, and there he believed that Jesus had to be found not among the dead but among the living (see Jn 20:8), in the hearts of those who believed.

84. What is the order and structure of the narratives in John's Gospel?

A double order is found in John's Gospel—one linear or horizontal and the other concentric or chiastic, with narratives that correspond to each other on both sides of a central revelation. It is similar to the order found in the passion in the story of Jesus before Pilate (see Jn 18:28—19:16), as will be seen later. It is probable that this order was introduced in the final edition of the Gospel.

In its initial redaction, the Gospel followed a horizontal order in its narrations. It started with an introduction (Jn 1:19—51), followed by the book of signs (Jn 2—12): From Cana to Cana (Jn 2:1—4:54); Jesus source of life in the feasts and the Jews (Jn 5:1—11:54); followed by the conclusion and evaluation of the ministry (Jn 12). The second part of the Gospel could be better called the book of the hour (since the glory of Jesus is revealed throughout the Gospel), although it is generally known as the book of glory (Jn 13—20). It covers the Last Supper (Jn 13—17), the passion (Jn 18—19), and the resurrection (Jn 20).

In its final edition (or redaction), material was added to the Gospel; the new material had a concentric structure centered on John 8:12, a verse that by reason of its position, would be the most important verse of the Gospel: "I am the light of the world. Whoever follows me will never walk in darkness but will have the light of life."

STRUCTURE OF
THE FOURTH GOSPEL

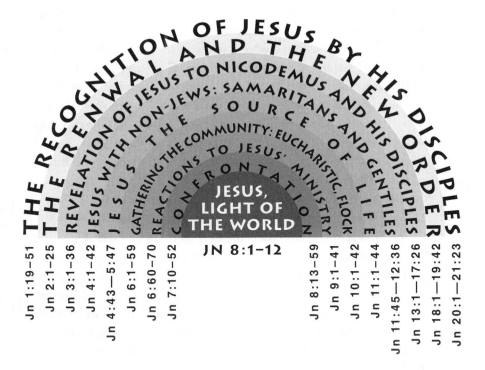

This concentric structure clearly shows how the sections correspond to each other in their themes and, at times, even in their vocabulary, so that the thought and intent of the author are clarified.

1. In the second chapter, the wedding feast at Cana and the purification of the Temple have their complement in the passion narrative. There the hour of Jesus announced in Cana finally arrives; the glory of Jesus is revealed in both narrations; and the mother of Jesus has a role in both sections. In the passion, the Jews destroy the temple of Jesus, of which he had spoken in chapter 2.

2. In the third chapter, with its double references to baptism (Jn 3:3, 5) and the interruption of the theme of the dialogue with Nicodemus as the last witness of John the Baptist (Jn 3:22–30), many detect evidence of later editing. The interview of Jesus with Nicodemus has corresponding parallels in the Last Supper discourse. In both sections, the necessity of water is mentioned at the beginning: for rebirth (in chapter 3) and for being washed by Jesus to take part with him in the supper. Jesus is the teacher, who teaches Nicodemus the teacher in Israel, and is also the teacher of his disciples at the supper. Nicodemus does not understand Jesus' words, just as Saint Peter does not understand what Jesus is trying to do, although Peter understands later. Nicodemus is told how God loved the world and sent his own Son, while at the Last Supper the disciples are told how the love of God the Father comes to the world—because the Father loves the Son, and the Son has loved his disciples, and the disciples will continue loving each other after the example of Jesus. In this way the world will experience the love of God, through the action of Christians.

3. In the sixth chapter, in the eucharistic discourse (Jn 6:31–59), initially the bread from heaven is the doctrine of Jesus (Jn 6:31–50); in the final section the food is the flesh and the blood of Jesus that he offers as a sacrifice of his own (Jn 6:51–59). Jesus gives a food that will satiate all hungers. In the parallel section of the Gospel, in the parable of the Good Shepherd (Jn 10:1–30), Jesus comes to gather his sheep in unity, to feed them, and to give his life for them. Both sections affirm the unity of the community that gathers around Jesus, so that no one is lost, and the sacrifice of Jesus for his own flock.

4. The eleventh chapter was possibly added at the end of the first century, in the final edition of the Gospel, together with the closely parallel sections of chapter 5 (Jn 5:25–29), to answer the possible

questions of some Christians who asked what was going to happen to those who died before the second coming of Jesus. The story of the resurrection of Lazarus assures them that those who are friends of Jesus should not be afraid of death, since death is nothing more than a sleep or a dream from which Jesus will come to awaken them. The parallelism between the central verses of these sections is remarkable (Jn 5:25 and Jn 11:25).

Attentive readers discover the many elements that correspond to each other in the sections of this concentric structure and are better able to understand the evangelist's intentions:

(a) *The recognition of Jesus by his disciples* (Jn 1:19–51)
  (b) *The renewal: Cana and the Temple* (Jn 2:1–25)
   (c) *Revelation of Jesus to Nicodemus* (Jn 3:1–36)
    (d) *Jesus and the Samaritans* (Jn 4:1–42)
     (e) *Jesus source of Life* (Jn 4:43—5:47)
      (f) *Multiplication of the bread;*
      eucharistic discourse (Jn 6:1–59)
       (g) *Responses to the mission of Jesus:*
       Jews, disciples, and relatives (Jn 6:60–70)
        (h) *Confrontation: The identity of Jesus* (Jn 7:1–52)
        (i) **JESUS, LIGHT OF THE WORLD** (Jn 8:12)
        (h') *Confrontation renewed* (Jn 8:13–59)
       (g') *The ideal response to Jesus* (Jn 9:1–41)
      (f') *The good and sacrificial shepherd* (Jn 10:1–42)
     (e') *Jesus restores life to Lazarus* (Jn 11:1–44)
    (d') *Jesus in Jerusalem: Gentiles with Jesus* (Jn 11:45—12:36)
   (c') *Revelation of Jesus to his disciples* (Jn 13:1—17:26)
  (b') *The new order: Process of Jesus; Calvary* (Jn 18—19)
(a') *The resurrection: Recognition of the risen Jesus* (Jn 20:1—21:23)

85. How does Saint John's Gospel differ from the synoptic Gospels?

Saint Clement of Alexandria referred to John's Gospel as the *spiritual Gospel,* because the material or physical facts of the ministry of Jesus were already contained in the synoptic Gospels. Saint John would have interpreted the sayings of Jesus in the light of the Holy Spirit after the Easter experience. Saint John's Gospel, much more than those of the synoptic writers, continues to be a universe in which new discoveries are found; it is a sky filled with stars in which new lights and stars are continuously being discovered.

The differences between Saint John's Gospel and the synoptic Gospels are evident with regard to the geography of the ministry of Jesus, the chronology, and the message preached:

	JOHN	SYNOPTICS
1. Geography	Jesus travels continuously between Galilee and Jerusalem.	Jesus travels through Galilee, in the north of Palestine, until he goes up to Jerusalem just once.
2. Chronology	The ministry seems last a little over two years, since he speaks of three Easter feasts.	The ministry lasts just one year, and Jesus goes up to Jerusalem only once for the passion.
3. Message	The person of Jesus, his actions, discourses, and controversies, together with the new commandment of love.	The kingdom of God, conversion, numerous commandments, teachings, and counsels to the disciples.

The Gospel of John has several narratives that parallel the synoptic Gospels: the vocation of the disciples, the expulsion of the vendors from the Temple, the healing of the paralytic, the multiplication of the bread, Jesus walking on the water, the confession of Peter, the healing of a blind man, the anointing of Jesus by a woman, and the passion and resurrection. Saint John has added the discourses to the miracles to explain the significance of Jesus' actions.

In the synoptic Gospels Jesus is the Messiah and a teacher who gives his disciples directions for the life they are to lead. Saint John presents Jesus as a person with whom his disciples must identify, a Jesus who, through the faith and love of his disciples, will continue to live in them. The disciples must learn to think, speak, and act like Jesus; they are going to be the continued incarnation of Jesus throughout history. Seeing a disciple must lead an observer to recognize Jesus in him, just as to see

Jesus leads to the knowledge of the Father who sent him and who lived in him (see Jn 14:10–11).

86. What are the most famous passages in Saint John's Gospel?

All the passages in which Jesus identifies himself have infinite value for believers: Jesus the Bread of Life, the Good Shepherd, the resurrection and the life, the way, the truth, and the life, and so on. Five texts in John's Gospel have special importance because of their message, their placement (position) in the Gospel, or their traditional influence in the life of practicing Catholics:

1. *The Word became flesh* (Jn 1:14): From the beginning of the Gospel's prologue, the evangelist reveals that Jesus is God made man, he who brings us salvation and grace. This text is used by the faithful in the recitation of the Angelus prayer.

2. *For God so loved the world that he gave his only Son, so that everyone who believes in him may not perish but may have eternal life* (Jn 3:16): This is a favorite and consoling verse, very popular among evangelical Christians; it is often used on posters and shirts for young people.

3. *I am the light of the world* (Jn 8:12): This is the central verse of the Gospel in its chiastic structure. Its importance can be seen also from the First Letter of Saint John, where we are told that the first basic revelation we received was that God is light (see 1 Jn 1:5).

4. *Here is your King!* (Jn 19:14): These words of Pilate in the passion have special importance for the evangelist. Pilate, unaware of it, was announcing the arrival of the King and the kingdom of God. Because of this Saint John points out the circumstances of the declaration of Pilate: in the place called the Stone Pavement or *Lithostrotos,* on the Day of Preparation for the Passover, at noon. When an event is important in the life of an individual, the circumstances are remembered.

5. *My Lord and my God!* (Jn 20:28): The profession of faith by Saint Thomas is the model of faith for those who find it difficult to believe. Many Catholics repeat the words of Saint Thomas when they look at the Eucharist during the consecration of the Mass.

87. What is the central idea or theme of the Gospel of Saint John?

Although John's Gospel has many ideas, all of which are important, two are most relevant for today's world: (1) Jesus is the light of the world, and (2) Christians are called to make Jesus present (to be representatives of Jesus) in our life and in our world.

Jesus, the Light of the World, shows us the way we must follow. The Book of Psalms spoke of the Law and the word of God as a light for life. Psalm 27 resonates in the Gospel of John; the man born blind and healed by Jesus can identify with the psalmist and say that

"The Lord is my light and my salvation" (Ps 27:1),
and that *"my adversaries and foes—they shall stumble
and fall"* (Ps 27:2), and *"if my father and mother forsake me,
the Lord will take me up"* (Ps 27:10).

Psalm 119:105 reminds us also that "Your Word is a lamp for my feet." The documents found in Qumran, near the Dead Sea, contain many allusions to light and truth—as something that defines authentic and faithful Jews. Jesus, our light, helps us to see and to distinguish the good from the bad. Without the light of Jesus we are in danger of stumbling (see Jn 11:9–11) and of guiding ourselves with the lights of the world that focus on idols, power, pleasures, and wealth. With the light of Jesus, a Christian can see the dangers that worldly values present for a truly Christian life.

In the prologue of John's Gospel, light is already a dominant theme repeated in verses 1:4, 5, 7, 8, and 9. In the dialogue of Jesus with Nicodemus, the theme of light summarizes the ministry of Jesus. In the conclusion of the book of signs, Saint John sums up the ministry of Jesus in terms of the light that came into the world and was not received or accepted (see Jn 11:37; 12:46).

In the central section of the Gospel (chapters 7 and 8) when the Jews keep trying to discover the true identity and mission of Jesus, the evangelist has placed verse 8:12 as the most vivid answer to their quest: "I am the light of the world. Whoever follows me will never walk in darkness but will have the light of life." This verse is considered by some commentators as an isolated pronouncement of Jesus, not directly related to its immediate context. However, it is important to notice that this verse holds the key answer to the questions presented in both chapters. The light of Jesus helps us understand his message, to see the hand of God in history and in the things that surround us, beginning with people and what happens to them.

The second key idea of John's Gospel is that Jesus lives and acts through those who believe in him. Jesus promised to return to be with us and in us. Faith and love are the guides that direct the efforts of a Christian to be like Jesus. In the three synoptic Gospels, a believer can read and learn what Jesus had said was to be done to become his faithful and obedient disciples. In the fourth Gospel, Saint John tells us the things that Jesus said and did, how he responded to challenges and to his enemies. Jesus is the model and example that a Christian must follow and imitate.

To be Jesus, or to be like Jesus, is a teaching shared by Saint John with Saint Paul. The message that Saint Paul received at his conversion was the realization that Jesus was identified with his disciples. Paul persecuted Christians believing he was being faithful to the Law of Moses. On the way to Damascus Paul learned that he was persecuting Jesus himself, since Jesus lived in those who had been baptized. Thus, Saint Paul says, "It is no longer I who live, but it is Christ who lives in me" (Gal 2:20). In John's Gospel the man born blind becomes another Jesus who argues with his enemies as the story progresses (see Jn 9:1–41).

88. What is the special significance of the famous prologue to John's Gospel (Jn 1:1–18)?

Many commentators think that the prologue of Saint John's Gospel initially could have been a wisdom hymn that the evangelist adapted and enriched to apply to Jesus as an introduction to his public ministry in this world. The adaptation of the preexisting hymn was made after the composition of the Gospel so that the hymn became a theological meditation on Jesus and his work as narrated in the rest of the Gospel. The prologue introduces the plan of salvation of God for his people and for all of humanity.

Others consider the prologue a Christian hymn with ideas similar to other hymns in the New Testament in which reference is made to the preexistence of Christ, his role in creation, his incarnation, and glorification (see Phil 2:6–11; Col 1:15–20, 3:16; Eph 5:19; 1 Tim 3:16).

The prologue contains a theological synthesis of the Christology of the Gospel and of God's plan in the history of salvation: Jesus, God with the Father; the preexistence of the Word; his role in the creation of the world and his relationship with humanity; his entrance into the history of the chosen people and in the life of believers; the divine filiation which Christians receive through him. The Word is truly God made man.

Many truths or teachings in John's Gospel have a place along the lines of the prologue, which becomes a true introduction to the Gospel itself. When a person introduces someone, the one making the introduction knows well the person being introduced and can speak with truth and authority about her or him; one cannot really introduce a stranger. The author of the adaptation of the prologue knew very well the contents of the rest of the Gospel.

With all this in mind we can affirm that the prologue of the Gospel was added when the Gospel received its final order and structure in the second redaction of the work. Possibly the Gospel, in its original presentation, began as a historical and theological record with a general reference to the preaching and testimony of John the Baptist, followed by the first testimony of John before the priests and Levites from Jerusalem asking him about his identity (see Jn 1:6–7, 19–34).

Many scholars study the prologue with few references to the affirmations that follow in the Gospel. They study very carefully the order and gradual development of the ideas expressed there and their roots in the Old Testament or in the Jewish theologies during that period. Others propose that the Gospel should be read in the light of the prologue; this is true, but the prologue also must be read in the light of the Gospel.

1. **"In the beginning was the Word, and the Word was with God, and the Word was God" (Jn 1:1).**

There are similar affirmations in the Gospel:

"...that the Father is in me and I am in the Father" (Jn 10:38).

"...that they may all be one. As you, Father, are in me and I am in you, may they also be in us, so that the world may believe that you have sent me. The glory that you have given me I have given them, so that they may be one, as we are one" (Jn 17:21–22).

"The Father and I are one" (Jn 10:30).

"So now, Father, glorify me in your own presence with the glory that I had in your presence before the world existed" (Jn 17:5).

"No one has ascended into heaven except the one who descended from heaven, the Son of Man" (Jn 3:13).

"Jews were seeking all the more to kill him, because he was not only breaking the sabbath, but was also calling God his own Father, thereby making himself equal to God" (Jn 5:18).

Jesus is the "I Am" (see Jn 18:5; 6:20; 8:28, 58; 13:19)

Many other texts can help us understand these words of the prologue. The numerous "I am" sayings echo the name of God revealed to Moses in Exodus (see Ex 3:13–15). Jesus knew what is within each person (see Jn 2:25); he is the Savior of the world (see Jn 4:42).

2. **"In him was life"** (Jn 1:4).
   There are similar affirmations in the Gospel:

   "The Son gives life to whomever he wishes" (Jn 5:21).

   "I am the way, and the truth, and the life" (Jn 14:6).

   "I am the resurrection and the life" (Jn 11:25).

   "Whoever believes in the Son has eternal life" (Jn 3:36).

   "I came that they may have life, and have it abundantly" (Jn 10:10).

3. **"Life was the light of all people. The light shines in the darkness, and the darkness did not overcome it." (Jn 1:4–5). "The true light, which enlightens everyone, was coming into the world. He was in the world, and the world came into being through him; yet the world did not know him" (Jn 1:9–10).**
   There are similar affirmations in the Gospel:

   "I am the light of the world. Whoever follows me will never walk in darkness but will have the light of life" (Jn 8:12).

   "He came to what was his own, and his own people did not accept him" (Jn 1:11).

   "As long as I am in the world, I am the light of the world" (Jn 9:5).

And this is the judgment, that the light has come into the world,
and people loved darkness rather than light
because their deeds were evil (Jn 3:19).

"I have come as light into the world, so that everyone who believes
in me should not remain in the darkness" (Jn 12:46).

"I, the light, have come into the world so that anyone who believes
in me will not remain in darkness" (Jn 12:46).

4. **"He came to what was his own, and his own people did not accept him"** (Jn 1:11).
   There are similar affirmations in the Gospel:

   "I have come in my Father's name, and you do not accept me;
   if another comes in his own name, you will accept him" (Jn 5:43).

   "If I had not come and spoken to them, they would not have sin;
   but now they have no excuse for their sin" (Jn 15:22).

   "For all who do evil hate the light and do not come to the light,
   so that their deeds may not be exposed" (Jn 3:20).

5. **"To those who received him, he gave them power to become Sons of God, those who believe in his name"** (Jn 1:12).
   There are similar affirmations in the Gospel:

   "I tell you, no one can see the kingdom of God
   without being born from above" (Jn 3:3).

   "I tell you, no one can enter the kingdom of God
   without being born of water and Spirit" (Jn 3:5).

   "Unless I wash you, you have no share with me" (Jn 13:8).

6. **"And the Word became flesh and lived among us, and we have seen his glory, the glory as of a father's only son, full of grace and truth"** (Jn 1:14).
   There are similar affirmations in the Gospel:

   "I came from the Father and have come into the world; again,
   I am leaving the world and am going to the Father" (Jn 16:28).

*"Jesus did this, the first of his signs, in Cana of Galilee,
and revealed his glory"* (Jn 2:11).

*""Did I not tell you that if you believed,
you would see the glory of God"* (Jn 11:40).

"The hour has come for the Son of Man to be glorified" (Jn 12:23).

*"Father, the hour has come; glorify your Son so that the Son
may glorify you"* (Jn 17:1).

*"So now, Father, glorify me in your own presence with the glory
that I had in your presence before the world existed"* (Jn 17:5).

"Grace and truth came through Jesus Christ" (Jn 1:17).

Calvary is the glorification of Jesus (see Jn 7:39).

89. What is the special message of the first week of Jesus ministry (Jn 1:19–51?)

Saint John offers a chronology of the first week of the ministry of Jesus in which some authors suggest a reference to the seven days of a new creation, thinking of the Book of Genesis and the creation of the world to which Saint John alludes in the opening words of the prologue. At the end of the Gospel, Saint John narrates two apparitions of Jesus in the first week after the resurrection.

In these narratives of the first week, Saint John wants to reveal the identity of Jesus gradually through a variety of titles. In addition, he wants to suggest that the birth of a New Israel is taking place, formed by the disciples of Jesus. We examine here the first four days of this week:

1. The first day (see Jn 1:19–28) reveals that Jesus is the one who is "in the midst" of the people; they have to discover who he is. After the resurrection, Jesus appears in the midst of his disciples (see Jn 20:19, 26). Mary Magdalene and the disciples find it difficult to recognize the risen Jesus (see Jn 20:15; 21:7). Mary thought she has seen the gardener; Thomas wanted to see the same physical Jesus as before, with the scars from the passion, not a Jesus transformed, with a different appearance; in the apparition of Jesus near the lake, after the miraculous catch of fish, only the beloved disciple was able to

identify Jesus. In Saint Luke's Gospel, the disciples think they have met a pilgrim walking along with them on the road, and later they think they see a ghost (see Lk 24:13–35, 37).

2. On the second day (see Jn 1:29–34), we find a number of revealing titles given to Jesus: the Lamb of God who takes away the sin of the world, the one who existed since before, the one who receives the Holy Spirit, the one who baptizes with the Holy Spirit, the Chosen One (Son) of God. All of these titles will be applied to the disciples after the resurrection.

3. The third day (see Jn 1:35–39) is decisive: a new community begins to be born with the first disciples who remain with Jesus. Importantly, on this day we have the first words of Jesus in the Gospel of John, words that are timely for anyone who wishes to follow Jesus: *"What are you looking for?"* These are also the first words of Jesus at the beginning of the passion (see Jn 18:4) and when Jesus rises from the dead (see Jn 20:15). These are the first words that the Church addresses to a person in the baptismal liturgy and to those who wish to enter religious life. This is, then, the first question that a Christian must ask at the beginning of any work or project.

4. On the fourth day (see Jn 1:40–42), Andrew, one of the two disciples who had followed Jesus, begins to give witness to Jesus by bringing his brother, Simon Peter, to the Lord. Andrew knew already that Jesus was the Messiah, because he had spent time with Jesus, even if only for a few hours (see Jn 1:39). For Saint John, one who lives with Jesus gets to know him deeply, as happens later with the inhabitants of Samaria, who after Jesus stayed with them for two days, could tell the Samaritan woman that Jesus was not just the Messiah, the savior of Israel, but that he was a Super-Messiah, the savior of the world (see Jn 4:40–42). Saint John does not say that Peter recognized Jesus; on the contrary, it was Jesus who recognized Peter and changed his name, to foretell the future mission of the apostle.

90. What is the message of Jesus' encounter with Nathanael (Jn 1:43–52)?

The fifth day of Jesus' ministry reveals several additional titles for Jesus: the son of Joseph, the one from Nazareth, the one about whom Moses wrote, the Son of God, the King of Israel, the Son of Man. Nathanael is a symbolic figure who personifies the New Israel that Jesus comes to gather and create. Nathanael is a true Israelite in whom there are no trickery or lies. He is the opposite of Jacob, of the Old Israel, who had been famous for his trickery (see Gen 25:29–34; 27:1–19; 30:25–43). Like those of the Old Israel, Nathanael and the other disciples will see the ladder that the old patriarch saw in Bethel, with angels ascending and descending (see Gen 28:10–17); the New Israel will not be less than the old one.

Nathanael had been under a fig tree, possible praying or meditating about something very personal; Jesus' revelation went straight to his heart. In the rabbinical tradition, the vine and the fig tree were two trees that Israelites should enjoy and have in their gardens. Some thought of these trees as the ones in Eden or paradise—the tree of life and the tree of knowledge of good and evil. Under the fig tree Nathanael could have been meditating on the coming of the long-desired Messiah.

When Nathanael heard the revelation from Jesus, he accorded Jesus the highest titles that a Jew could give to a living person: *Son of God* and *King of Israel* (see Jn 1:49). At the end of the Gospel, in the parallel narrative, the apostle Thomas addresses Jesus with the two highest titles that a Christian believer could give to Jesus: *My Lord* and *my God!* (see Jn 20:28). The title of Jesus as *King of Israel* prepares the way for the narrative in Cana as the arrival of the kingdom of God.

It is important to note the parallelism created by the evangelist in the structures of the two complementary sections of his Gospel: the stories of Nathanael and Thomas (Jn 1:43–51; 20:24–29):

1. Their friends give them witness about Jesus.
2. Nathanael and Thomas refuse to believe: *From Nazareth? If I do not see and touch I will not believe.*
3. Jesus makes to each of them a personal and intimate revelation: *I saw you under the fig tree; Jesus has heard the conditions presented by Thomas.*
4. Greatest confession of faith of each one: *Son of God, King; My Lord and my God.*
5. Jesus questions each on the reason for their faith: *Because I told you? Because you have seen me?*
6. Announcement for the future: *You will see greater things; believe without seeing.*

Two days after the meeting with Nathanael, the Wedding Feast of Cana takes place; it closes the first week of ministry and announces the arrival of the kingdom.

91. What is the special message of the first miracle of Jesus at the Wedding Feast of Cana (Jn 1:1–11)?

Jesus' first miracle at Cana is a programmatic miracle that announces and sums up the entire ministry of Jesus. It introduces and announces the kingdom of God. In the synoptic Gospels, the kingdom is compared to a wedding feast that a king had for his son (see Mt 22:1–4). Saint John gives us a similar message through this narration of the wedding. The kingdom has arrived and demands a conversion.

At Cana, Jesus performs a marvelous conversion that is nothing but a sign of what Jesus really seeks to accomplish through his message. Saint John does not speak at length about the kingdom in his Gospel except in the dialogue with Nicodemus (see Jn 3:3–5). At the end of the Gospel, in the parallel section of the passion, he solemnly announces the arrival of the King, through the declaration of Pilate, which is discussed later.

The two narratives in the second chapter of John—the wedding feast and the cleansing of the Temple—correlate with their parallel section in the later account of the passion. There, once again, the mother of Jesus will be present, the hour of Jesus will come, the full glorification of Jesus that started at Cana will take place, and the Temple of which Jesus had spoken will be destroyed.

Jesus' first miracle takes on added symbolism and meaning from the second miracle, which also takes place at Cana (see Jn 4:46–54), although the healing in the second miracle happens in Capernaum, at a distance. The message of both miracles is the same: Jesus comes to transform and perform conversion in the religious world, in the institutions, and in people. In the second sign, the real miracle occurs in the change and transformation of the royal official-man-father in the measure by which his faith increases.

John frequently offers clues to his thinking at the beginning and at the end of some of his narratives. The clues at Cana suggest a symbolic interpretation. The miracle happens on the third day, in a wedding feast, in the presence and activity of the mother of Jesus. At the end of the narration, John says that this was the first of the signs through which Jesus revealed his glory and that the disciples responded with faith.

The miracle takes place on the third day after the former narration; in the tradition of the Old Testament, the third day is a day of revelation (see Ex 19:10–16). In Jesus' case, the third day will be one of resurrection and new life. In the Old Testament, a wedding was a symbol of the relationship of God with his people, of the sacred covenant they had made. Saint John may want us to think here of the new covenant that Jesus is bringing. As noted, in the synoptic Gospels a wedding is a symbol of the kingdom of God. The presence of the mother of Jesus in this miracle is so important that without her no miracle would have taken place. Jesus demands faith from those who ask for a miracle (see Jn 4:48); this faith was expressed by Mary with her implicit petition.

Pope Paul VI, at the end of his Apostolic Exhortation for the Right Ordering and Development of Devotion to the Blessed Virgin Mary (*Marialis Cultus,* 56), suggests that Saint John is announcing the beginning of a new covenant at Cana, reading it in the light of the Exodus covenant (see Ex 19:8; 24:3, 7; Dt 5:25). In Exodus, as in Cana, people must do whatever the Lord says; it will be on the third day that the glory of God will appear on Sinai; and the purpose of the revelation to Moses will be that people will believe him forever.

At the end of the narration, Saint John says that this miracle was a sign, the first one; a sign is directed *toward* something more important and points toward something that is not yet seen. Smoke is a sign that there must be also fire; the sound of a siren indicates that there might be an accident or a crime. This sign of Jesus reveals that Jesus was coming to change something more than water into wine; through faith, he was going to change the hearts of people; he was going to substitute the whole system of external purifications centered around the Temple of Jerusalem.

Saint John says that the servers at the wedding feast—the deacons— obeyed the orders of Jesus, filling the jars with water and bringing it to the head steward. John adds that the servers knew where the wine came from because they had taken it out. For Saint John, one of the ways to get to know Jesus and know the origin of his doctrine and gifts is to do what he says, to obey his commandments (see Jn 7:17). The servers had obeyed Jesus, as later will do those who believe in him; because of their faith, they will be able to give witness about him.

92. Why is the "hour" of Jesus so important in John's Gospel (Jn 2:4)?

The fourth Gospel has seven special references to the "hour" of Jesus; they are so ordered that the message of the evangelist becomes increasingly evident:

(1) Jn 2:4: *My hour has not yet come.*
    (2) Jn 7:30: *They tried to arrest him....**his hour had not yet come.***
        (3) Jn 8:20: *No one arrested him,* **because his hour had not yet come.**
            (4) Jn 12:23: ***The hour has come*** *for the Son of Man to be glorified.*
        (5) Jn 13:1: *Jesus, knowing that **the hour had come**...*
    (6) Jn 17:1: *Father, **the hour has come**...*
(7) Jn 19:27: ***From that hour*** *the disciple took her into his own home.*

The first and the last mentions of the "hour" is associated with the presence and mission of Mary: when Jesus is rendering a great service to the marrying couple and when Mary is called to the service of the disciples of Jesus. The second and the third mentions of the "hour" have a correspondence in the fifth and the sixth mentions.

In the center of the texts related to the "hour" of Jesus, the evangelist reveals his intention by carefully creating a concentric structure, just as he does in other sections of the Gospel (see John 12:23–28):

(a) *The* **hour** *has come for the Son of Man to be* **glorified**   GLORY
  (b) *Unless a grain of wheat falls into the earth and **dies***
    *Those who love their life **lose it**, and those who hate*
      their life in this world will keep it for eternal life   PASSION
      (c) *Whoever **serves** me **must follow me**,*
        *and where I am, there will my **servant** be also.*
      *Whoever **serves** me, the Father will honor.*   SERVICE
    (b') *Now my soul is troubled....should I say—*
  *"Father, **save me from this hour**?"*   PASSION
  (a') *It is for this reason that I have come to this **hour**.*
*Father, **glorify** your name.*   GLORY

This structural arrangement shows that the hour of Jesus (and that of a Christian) is a mixture of suffering and joy, something glorious and painful, as it is to die and to lose one's life. The text reminds us of Jesus' petition in the agony in the garden as narrated in the synoptic Gospels. The central verse of this section repeats three times the same Greek verb *diakoneo* (to serve) because the hour of Jesus and of a Christian arrives when one is called to service. In his passion Jesus rendered the greatest service to humanity. When Christians are offered an opportunity to serve, then their hour comes; this hour can be something painful, but when it is motivated by love, it becomes something glorious.

In John's story of the Last Supper, he alludes to the hour of a woman (in labor and childbirth; see Jn 16:21); when this time arrives, a woman's life changes radically. It is a painful and a glorious moment. The hour comes for the woman to serve, to live not just for herself but for someone else; she becomes a *mother* with everything that word evokes. Mary becomes a mother on Calvary once again at the foot of the cross. Her hour arrives then and coincides with the hour of Jesus. From that time forward, Mary is to live for the disciples of Jesus, for us who are her children.

93. Why did Jesus expel the vendors from the Temple (Jn 2:13–22)?

Saint John places the cleansing of the Temple at the beginning of his Gospel, whereas in the synoptic Gospels the event takes places when Jesus enters Jerusalem on Palm Sunday. In the synoptic Gospels, Jesus' action provokes the anger of the Jewish leaders who decide to eliminate Jesus. In Saint John's Gospel, the expulsion of the vendors announces what will take place in the passion when the Jews destroy the Temple, which is the body of Jesus.

In the synoptic Gospels, Jesus goes to Jerusalem only one time— for the passion. Thus, they were forced to place the expulsion of the merchants on that occasion. In John's Gospel, Jesus goes to Jerusalem multiple times, so John had a choice on where to place the incident in accordance with his theology. In the concentric order of the Gospel, the expulsion of the merchants corresponds to the passion; hence, we find the same type of connection as found in the synoptic Gospels where the accusation of the destruction of the Temple is part of the accusation of the Jews in the trial of Jesus.

Saint John includes a quote from Psalm 69:9, but he changes the tense of the verb. In the psalm, it is a past tense ("It is zeal for you has that *has consumed* me"), and John makes it future tense: "Zeal for your house *will consume* me" (Jn 2:17; emphases added). The quote now announces that the death of Jesus will be a consequence of his ministry.

The second chapter of Saint John's Gospel, with the wedding feast and the cleansing of the Temple, also announces that Jesus comes to substitute and replace the Jewish religious system. Access to God will not depend on ritual purifications or on a Temple built by human hands. Jesus will be the new temple in which the new community will gather. In Jesus they will be purified. The true adorers of the Father are going to adore in spirit and truth, in the new temple that is Jesus (see Jn 4:20–24).

Jesus is the new spiritual temple of the Israel of God. From the right side of the temple (like from the Temple of Jerusalem in the vision of the prophet Ezekiel) rivers of living water will flow forth as the source of life for believers (see Jn 7:37–39; Ez 47:1–2; Zech 14:8).

94. What is the message of Jesus' dialogue with Nicodemus (Jn 3:1–36)?

The dialogue of Jesus with the Pharisee Nicodemus in chapter 3 of John's Gospel parallels the teachings of Jesus to his disciples during the Last Supper. Both sections of the Gospel are organized in a similar pattern:

JOHN 3	JOHN 13—17
Jesus dialogues with Nicodemus (Jn 3:1–21).	Jesus washes the feet of the disciples; first section of the discourse (Jn 13:1—15:10).
Last witness of John the Baptist (Jn 3:22–30).	Second section of the discourse (Jn 15:12—16:33).
Commentary of the evangelist (Jn 3:31–36).	Priestly prayer of Jesus (Jn 17:1–26).

An important idea that links both sections of the Gospel is the perfect joy Jesus wants for his disciples:

- 3:29: "The friend of the bridegroom, who stands and hears him, rejoices greatly at the bridegroom's voice. For this reason my joy has been fulfilled."
- 15:11: "I have said these things to you so that my joy may be in you, and that your joy may be complete."
- 17:13: "I am coming to you, and I speak these things in the world so that they may have my joy made complete in themselves."

The dialogue begins by announcing the need to be born again in order to belong to the kingdom of God. The Last Supper opens with the washing of the feet and the need for Peter to be washed in order to be part of Jesus and be one of his disciples. Nicodemus does not understand the initial message of Jesus, just as Peter does not understand Jesus, although Peter will understand later (see Jn 13:7).

Nicodemus is presented as a teacher of the law (see Jn 3:1, 10), although Jesus is the only true teacher (see Jn 13:12–15). Nicodemus is told that one must be born of the Spirit and let oneself be guided by it (see Jn 3:5, 9); Saint Peter will have to obey Jesus by letting him wash his feet. Jesus makes a double promise of the Spirit who will instruct the disciples and guide them in their mission to the world (see Jn 14:15–26; 16:4–15).

Jesus announces to Nicodemus, in general terms, the immense love of God: "For God so loved the world that he gave his only Son, so that everyone who believes in him may not perish but may have eternal life" (Jn 3:16). At the Last Supper Jesus reveals how the love of God comes to the world through certain close channels: Jesus is the first channel of God's revelation and love: "As the Father has loved me, so I have loved you; abide in my love" (Jn 15:9). Jesus transmits the love of the Father to the disciples who will love as Jesus has loved. It is through them that the love of God will come to the world and will be a witness to the Father and to Jesus. Love, faith ,and obedience to Jesus will result in the fullness of joy for the disciples (see Jn 15:11).

Jesus also announces to Nicodemus that the response to the love of God will not always be positive; those who reject the light and refuse to believe, they remain in darkness and do not wish that their conduct be exposed or denounced (see Jn 3:18–21). At the Last Supper Jesus announces that the Holy Spirit, the Spirit of Truth, will come to expose and denounce the sin and lack of faith of the world that will reject his message (as Jn 16:4–11).

The witness of John the Baptist that interrupts the dialogue with Nicodemus presents John the Baptist as the first disciple and witness to Jesus. Because John is totally consecrated to Jesus and his mission and gives witness to him, John the Baptist already experiences the fullness of joy (see Jn 3:22–30). At the Last Supper the disciples are the ones called to give witness to Jesus, to live with and for Jesus, so that they will also experience the fullness of joy that Jesus desires for his own (see Jn 15:11; 17:13).

At the end of the dialogue it is not clear whether Nicodemus has become a disciple of Jesus. Nicodemus appears again later (in Jn 7:50–52), defending Jesus but without professing openly that he is a believer.

95. What is the message of the story of the Samaritan woman (Jn 4)?

The dialogue of Jesus with the woman from Samaria announces the conversion of the entire town or people represented by the woman. The people of Samaria accepted Christianity at a very early age (see Acts 8:4–8). The Samaritans were the first great harvest of the church.

The Gospel underscores, first of all, the superiority of Jesus and his gifts over the Old Testament: the water, the Temple, and the true adoration of God. A most important aspect of the dialogue is the process of conversion and growth in faith that occurs in the woman and in her people. The woman is an incarnation of the Samaritan nation, which had been integrated by five groups or tribes, each one with its religious "husband" or god. Later the Samaritans had begun to adore the God of Israel, but not in accordance with the legal prescriptions of the Old Testament (see 2 Kgs 17:24-41); hence, the God of Israel was not a true "husband" of the Samaritans.

The evangelist emphasizes the growth in the woman's faith through a series of titles that she bestows on Jesus. As the woman proceeds in discovering the identity of Jesus, she goes on to discover her own personal identity. There is a clear progression in the titles of Jesus and the responses of the woman to them:

JESUS	SAMARITAN
You, a Jew	I, a Samaritan
The gift of God (Jn 3:16)	Ignorant
The One asking	Inferior
Sir (Kyrie), from where	Inferior
Sir (Kyrie), give me	Inferior
Prophet	Sinner
Messiah	Messenger, apostle
Savior of the World	Disciple

The life of faith is a process of getting to know God and of knowing oneself. One who lives with Jesus comes to know him more deeply. Jesus, we are told, remained with the Samaritans for two days; since they lived with him, they could tell the woman that Jesus was much more than what she had announced, for Jesus was the Savior, not just of the Jews but of the whole world.

In the central section of the dialogue, Jesus reveals that true adorers of the Father are not going to adore in material temples but in Jesus, around whom and in whom the new community of believers will gather. The (true) adorers will appear again in the parallel section of the Gospel when Jesus enters into Jerusalem on Palm Sunday (see Jn 12:20). There, some foreigners, non-Jews like the Samaritans, approach Jesus through faith and Jesus announces solemnly the arrival of his "hour" of glory (Jn 12:23–28).

In this dialogue Jesus identifies himself for the first time with a divine title, "I AM," declaring that he is the Messiah. In making his revelation, Jesus chose not a man but a woman, not a Jew but a pagan, not a holy person, but a sinner. Jesus went against all prejudices of his time: racial, social, and ethical.

96. What is the relationship of Jesus' second miracle with his first miracle (Jn 4:46–54)?

The first section of the ministry of Jesus has been entitled by many *"From Cana to Cana."* The miracle of the son of the royal official in Saint John's Gospel is probably the evangelist's version of the healing of the son of the Roman centurion of the synoptics (see Mt 8:5-13; Lk 7:1-10). The father is a pagan, a model of faith; Jesus performs the miracle from a distance, without going personally to heal the sick person. The centurion of the synoptics is a model of faith from the beginning of the narration, while the official in Saint John's text is a model at the end of the process of faith that happens gradually in him.

The story of the royal official, the second miracle of Jesus, calls us to remember the first miracle at Cana. At the beginning of the narrative, the evangelist tells us that *"Jesus came again to Cana in Galilee where he had changed water into wine"* (Jn 4:46). At the end he reminds us again that *"this was the second sign that Jesus made when he returned from Judea to Galilee"* (Jn 4:54). The evangelist wants us to read the second sign in the light of the first.

The two miracles of Cana have for their theme the conversion that must accompany the arrival of the kingdom of God. In the second chapter, the subject is a religious conversion that goes beyond the ritual practices of purification and attendance at the temple. In the second miracle of Cana, conversion is an interior change of the personality, operated and guided by faith. It is worth pointing out the titles that the evangelist gives to the petitioner of the miracle as he grows in faith:

1. Royal Official   *"You will not believe"* (Jn 4:48)
2. The Man   *"Believed and went"* (Jn 4:50)
3. The Father   *"He himself believed, along with his whole household"* (Jn 4:53)

The changes in the name of the individual suggest a change in his personality. Where there is no faith, titles or rank and diplomas are all important. Faith starts by "humanizing" the person, since an inhuman person really has no faith, even if that person uses the name of God in speech. The perfect faith of the man, when he realized the miracle done by Jesus, made him truly be the father of his family, responsible for the material and spiritual well-being of his own.

In this miracle, Jesus gave life to the child who was near death, but we must realize that the person who really received life was the father, through a new and marvelous conversion. When a person is truly converted and begins to grow in faith, there should be a gradual change of personality and relationships, beginning with those that affect the members of one's family.

This narrative, like others in John's Gospel, serves as a hinge to close the cycle of conversion from Cana to Cana and to open the new cycle of Jesus as the source of life (see Jn 5–11).

97. What is the special significance of the healing of the paralytic by the pool (Jn 5:1–18)?

The third miracle of Jesus presents the healing of a man who is physically healed in his body but who is not changed in his heart and at the end joins the enemies of Jesus in the Temple: "Later Jesus found him in the temple and said to him, 'See, you have been made well! Do not sin any more, so that nothing worse happens to you'" (Jn 5:14). Here, John is not dealing with a providential illness with no relationship to sin, as will be the case of the man born blind whom Jesus later heals (see Jn 9:1–41). This paralytic man has an illness related to his own sins.

The paralytic man is a symbolic figure. The thirty-eight years of his illness recall the condition of the people of Israel during the Exodus, after their sin of murmuring in the desert, refusing to go ahead to the Promised Land (see Nm 14; Dt 1:35). In the Exodus narrative, all the adults who had come out from Egypt were condemned to die in the desert without seeing the Promised Land. The sin of the people occurred during the second year after they left Egypt. That rebellious generation had to wait for thirty-eight years, lost in the desert without hope, waiting only for death (see Dt 2:14–15).

The paralytic by the pool had also been blind (without hope) for thirty-eight years until Jesus came into his life. The man's illness, like the condition of Israel in the desert, was due to his sins. The man was healed in his body but not in his heart, for as noted, at the end of the miracle narrative, the man went to the Jews and gave them information about Jesus. The Lord found him in the Temple, the place where the Jews met and were to be found (see Jn 5:14–15). "[Jesus] came to what was his own, and his own people did not accept him" (Jn 1:11).

It is remarkable that in these two parallel sections of the Gospel in which Jesus gives life—first by healing the paralytic and later by bringing Lazarus back to life—the Jews respond by planning to kill Jesus (see Jn 5:16–18; 11:53; 12:10).

98. What does John's Gospel say about eschatology? What happens after a person's death?

Jesus' discourse after the healing of the paralytic man by the pool of Bethesda and Lazarus' resurrection presuppose a present or realized eschatology. Jews expected judgment and resurrection of the dead at the end of time or at the end of the present age. The final age of history has arrived with Jesus. Judgment takes place here and now; the resurrection happens now through faith. After the healing of the man born blind, Jesus is revealed as the Son of Man who has come for a judgment that is already happening (see Jn 9:39). The judgment will reach its climax in the passion, in the hour of Jesus (see Jn 12:31–32).

It is important to compare the different stages of the development of eschatology in John's Gospel as it appears in the healing of the paralytic and in the resurrection of Lazarus:

- 5:24: *Very truly, I tell you, anyone who hears my word and believes him who sent me has eternal life, and does not come under judgment, but has passed from death to life.*
- 5:25: *Very truly, I tell you, the hour is coming, and is now here, when the dead will hear the voice of the Son of God, and those who hear will live.*
- 5:28: *Do not be astonished at this; for the hour is coming when all who are in their graves will hear his voice.*
- 11:25: *I am the resurrection and the life. Those who believe in me, even though they die, will live.*
- 11:38–44: *Jesus...came to the tomb....He cried with a loud voice, "Lazarus, come out!" The dead man came out.*

In these verses the double redaction of the Gospel is evident. In John 5:24, Jesus speaks in the first-person singular, and eternal life and resurrection have started to happen with the preaching of Jesus. Verse 5:25 seems to have been added in the second redaction of the Gospel; the evangelist speaks of Jesus as the Son of God and seems to accept the futuristic eschatology of the synoptic Gospels. Verse 5:28 evokes the resurrection of Lazarus, when Jesus, near the sepulcher, will cry out loudly and Lazarus will rise and come out of the tomb.

Jesus' preaching demands a response from listeners. The response determines the judgment of the person. Jesus said, "I came into this world for judgment so that those who do not see may see, and those who do see may become blind" (Jn 9:39). The response of faith in Jesus is centered on his glorification and exaltation in the cross; everyone must make a decision for or against the crucified Jesus: "Now is the judgment of this world; now the ruler of this world will be driven out. And I, when I am lifted up from the earth, will draw all people1 to myself" (Jn 12:31–32). Everyone must look and see the one who was crucified and make a faith decision (see Jn 19:37).

Death, judgment, and eternal life are realities that start to happen now through faith in Jesus. Physical death will just be like a dream, or sleep, from which Jesus awaken his friends.

99. What is the meaning of the multiplication of the bread, and how is Jesus the Bread of Life (Jn 6:1–59)?

The multiplication of the bread is the most meaningful miracle of Jesus; it is narrated in all the Gospels. From the beginning the Church saw in it a foreshadowing of the Eucharist. Saint John has added a long discourse to explain the meaning of the miracle. Many scholars suspect that the last section of the discourse (see Jn 6:51–58), the sacramental section that speaks of eating the flesh and drinking the blood of Jesus, was added in the second redaction of the Gospel.

After the miracle of the multiplication of the bread, as in the synoptic Gospels (see Mk 6:45–52 and parallel), Jesus comes to meet his disciples in the middle of the sea and pronounces the revelatory words "I AM." Jesus is the I AM who had fed the people just as God had done during Exodus. Saint Mark adds after the multiplication that "they did not understand about the loaves, but their hearts were hardened" (Mk 6:52). It seems that the disciples had not understood that in the miracle of Jesus, God once again had fed his people as in the past. Saint John puts it clearly. The Jews were looking for an easy and cheap food that would make their life easier. The food for Jesus was to do the will of the Father (see Jn 4:34). The food now offered is the person and doctrine of Jesus that must be received and lived through faith.

The eucharistic discourse of Jesus follows the pattern of discourses used by Jewish rabbis. It begins with a quote from Scripture that is explained throughout the discourse (just as it is done in formal homilies in our parishes). The quote explained in the discourse literally states:

"He rained down on them manna to eat, and gave them the grain of heaven" (Psalm 78:24).

In the first part of the discourse (Jn 6:31–40), Jesus explains that the one who now gives bread from heaven is the Father who had fed his people during Exodus. In the central section (6:41–43), the evangelist affirms that Jesus is now the true bread from heaven that gives life to the receiver. This identification of Jesus is not accepted by the Jews because they think they know Jesus well; the evangelist expresses this through a verbal structure (emphases added):

Then the Jews *began to complain* about him because he said,
"I am the bread that *came down from heaven.*"
They were saying, *"Is not this Jesus, the son of Joseph?...*
How can he now say, 'I have *come down from heaven*'?"
Jesus answered them, "Do not *complain* among yourselves" (Jn 6:41–43).

The last section is sacramental (see Jn 6:51–58) and suggests that the readers of John's Gospel were in the habit of celebrating the Eucharist in their community with the elements of bread and wine that were consecrated in a manner similar to the one that until now has been preserved in the Catholic Church. To the ears of Jews, the words of Jesus were scandalous—to eat flesh and drink blood! For Christians these words affirmed their sacrament. The last section uses the future tense of verbs, and Jesus himself is the one who will give the food. In the first section of the discourse, the verbs are in the present tense, and it is the Father who gives the Bread of Life. In the final section, Jesus will give his flesh and blood through his sacrifice in Calvary (see Jn 6:51–58).

100. What should we know about the responses of people to the eucharistic sermon of Jesus? What is the *Galilean crisis?*

After the discourse on the Bread of Life, the evangelist presents the responses of people to the message of Jesus. First he speaks of the scandal of many of his disciples and their resistance to believe his words. He specifically points out that Judas was one of those who refused to believe (see Jn 6:64); then he relates the confession of Peter, who recognizes that Jesus is the only source of salvation and eternal life. The section concludes with a new reference to Judas, the betrayer (see Jn 6:70–71), Thus the profession of faith of Peter is contrasted with the two allusions to Judas. In the passion, the denials of Peter are contrasted with the testimony of Jesus before the high priest, Annas (see Jn 18:15–27).

The eucharistic discourse of Jesus results in the desertion of many of his disciples. Only the twelve apostles remain faithful to Jesus, although we are told that Judas was one of those who did not believe. The lack of faith is the reason why, one year later, Judas will betray the Lord.

The desertion of the disciples seems to be reflected in Saint Mark's and the other synoptic Gospels, where Jesus, after the confession of Peter, seems to limit his ministry to the instruction of the twelve apostles to prepare them to understand and accept the significance of the passion and its consequences for the lives of the disciples. This change of focus in the ministry of Jesus after the desertion of so many has been called the *Galilean crisis*.

The Catholic Church celebrates and professes the teachings of Jesus on the Eucharist in the celebration of the Mass. In the liturgy, the Church offers the faithful the bread of the Word, followed by the sacramental offering of the body and blood of Jesus which, when received with faith, brings the believer to an intimate communion with Jesus.

101. Who is Jesus? Why are there conflicts about his identity (Jn 7—8)?

The seventh and eighth chapters of Saint John's Gospel have their background in the Jewish Feast of Tabernacles, which was celebrated between September and October. This feast celebrated the miracles God had performed in favor of his people during the Exodus: water from the rock, and the column of fire that protected and guided the people during their pilgrimage. The women's courtyard of the Temple of Jerusalem was brightly illuminated with great candlesticks, lamps, and torches. This was also an agricultural feast, after the gathering of grapes and late fruits, when they prayed for rain for the autumn sowing.

This central section of John's Gospel recalls the controversies of Jesus with the Pharisees in the synoptic Gospels. John's text also includes the responses of the Christian community to the attacks of the neighboring Jewish communities against Jesus as Messiah. Is it possible that there was also a conflict with some Jews who had accepted Jesus as the Messiah announced by the prophets, but they refused to accept Jesus as the Son of God? They would be told that they will truly be disciples of Jesus when they believe in him fully, accepting the full truth about Jesus, and then they will enjoy true freedom. One who rejects Jesus remains a slave of the devil.

The recurring question in this section deals with Jesus' identity. At the center of these controversies, Jesus makes the most important revelation of the Gospel on his identity: *Jesus is the light of the world.* A fundamental truth for a Christian is that God is light and that Jesus is God (see 1 Jn 1:5).

In these two chapters, Saint John has created several parallels:

- 7:30: *Then they tried to arrest him, but no one laid hands on him, because his hour had not yet come.*
- 8:20: *...but no one arrested him, because his hour had not yet come.*
- 7:35: *The Jews said to one another, "Where does this man intend to go that we will not find him? Does he intend to go to the Dispersion among the Greeks and teach the Greeks? What does he mean by saying, 'You will look for me, and you will not find me. Where I will be you cannot come.'"*
- 8:21: *Again he said to them, "I am going away, and you will search for me, but you will die in your sin. Where I am going, you cannot come."*
- 7:36: *What does he mean by saying, 'You will search for me and you will not find me' and 'Where I am, you cannot come'?"*
- 8:22: *Then the Jews said, "Is he going to kill himself? Is that what he means by saying, 'Where I am going, you cannot come'?"*
- 7:18: *"Those who speak on their own seek their own glory; but the one who seeks the glory of him who sent him is true, and there is nothing false in him."*
- 8:50: *"Yet I do not seek my own glory; there is one who seeks it and he is the judge."*
- 7:19–24: The Jews are associated with Moses.
- 8:37–41: The Jews are associated with Abraham.

In this section, Jesus is first compared with Moses; at the end, Jesus is greater than Abraham. The old patriarch had given an example of faith and blind obedience to God, being ready even to sacrifice his only son.

The Father now has offered his own Son as a sacrifice. The Jews now do the opposite of what Abraham did—they refuse to believe that Jesus is the source of living water and the light of life. The revelation of Jesus will make sense only after his glorification in the cross, when Jesus will give the Spirit of light and life.

102. What does it mean that Jesus is the light of the world (Jn 8:12)?

The Feast of Tabernacles or booths celebrated the memory of the survival of the people during the forty-year pilgrimage through the Sinai desert. The column of fire that led the people and the water from the rock were special themes of the celebration. The entire city of Jerusalem was lit for the feast. Jesus is a greater and brighter light, for he shines for the whole world to see.

The last day of the festival, Jesus had revealed himself as the fountain of living water. Now Jesus declares himself as the light of life for all those who follow him. Already in the prologue of the Gospel, the evangelist had stated that "...*the life was the light of all people*" (Jn 1:4). Jesus had come to invite everyone to become children of the light (see Jn 12:36).

In this central verse of the Gospel, Saint John (8:12) combines some of the most important vocabulary used in his work; the words of this verse are much more commonly used by John than by the synoptic Gospel writers.

I am

the light

of the world.

Whoever

follows me

will never walk

in darkness but

will have the light

of life.

In the prologue and throughout John's Gospel, the acceptance or rejection of the light of Jesus was a deciding factor in the relationship with Jesus: "The true light, which enlightens everyone, was coming into the world" (Jn 1:9). "And this is the judgment, that the light has come into the world, and people loved darkness rather than light because their deeds were evil" (Jn 3:19). "For all who do evil hate the light and do not come to the light" (Jn 3:20).

Jesus' public ministry is summarized in terms of response to his light: "Jesus said to them, 'The light is with you for a little longer. Walk while you have the light, so that the darkness may not overtake you. If you walk in the darkness, you do not know where you are going. While you have the light, believe in the light, so that you may become children of light'" (Jn 12:35–36). "I have come as light into the world, so that everyone who believes in me should not remain in the darkness" (Jn 12:46).

Jesus is the light of the world while he is in the world (see Jn 9:5). The miracle of the man born blind with which Jesus affirms his words is just a sign of the divine light that guides the believer. The person who has the light of Christ in his or her heart with his or her personality and conduct radiates the Lord.

As noted previously in discussing John's prologue, the theme of light appears multiple times in the Old Testament in the Psalms and in Wisdom writings; it is also an important theme in the Dead Sea Scrolls. Among the Jews, the "light for the world" rested in the Law of Moses, the Temple, Jerusalem, and Israel. The word of the Lord is a light that shows the right way that must be followed. The servant of the Lord will be a light for the nations (see Is 42:6; 49:6). The light of God enables us to walk in the way of the Lord, allowing us to see and appreciate the beauty of God's creation, and helping us discover the hand of God in our life. It also shows us the dangers that we must avoid. Our disoriented world, more than ever, needs Jesus, the Light.

103. What is the symbolism of the healing of the man born blind (Jn 9:1–41)?

The healing of the man born blind is an early catechesis or instruction on the meaning of Christian baptism. What happens to the blind man is what happens to every Christian who comes into the world (Saint Augustine). The question here is not whether the blind man had sinned or not; his blindness looked to the future, not to the past. He was born so that the works of God would be revealed in him. The blind man also exemplifies the lot of those who converted to the new faith from Judaism; they were expelled from the synagogues. The blind man, when he washed himself according to Jesus' instruction, was so changed and transformed that his neighbors did not recognize him. Only when he opened his mouth did they discover the new identity he had received; the blind man kept saying: *"I AM."* He spoke like Jesus in the rest of the Gospel because he had become another Jesus; he had become a Christian. One could say here, with Saint Paul, that anyone washed by Christ has become a new person, for "It is no longer I who live, but it is Christ who lives in me" (Gal 2:20).

Saint John shows the process of development of faith in the man born blind; at the beginning of the narrative he knew almost nothing of Jesus, but at the end he recognized Jesus as the Son of Man (see Jn 9:35). This process of faith formation shares similarities with the story of the Samaritan woman (Jn 4):

THE SAMARITAN		THE BLIND MAN
You, a Jew	I, a Samaritan	That man called Jesus (Jn 9:11)
Sir (Kyrie)	She is ignorant	He does not know where Jesus is (Jn 9:12)
Sir, give me	She is inferior	(He is from God) (Jn 9:16)
Prophet	She, a sinner	Prophet (Jn 9:17)
Messiah	Messenger	Messiah (Jn 9:22)
Savior		
of the world	Disciple	Son of Man (Jn 9:35)

At the end of the narration, the blind man is expelled from the synagogue; this happened to the Jew who converted to the new faith when John was writing his Gospel. But the blind man was not left alone and isolated. Jesus found him and brought him to the end of his process of faith. Jesus is the Son of Man who even now is already judging the world. Everyone must make a decision for Jesus or for darkness. The world of darkness (of politics and dirty business, and so forth) until now continues to exclude and expel those who are true Christians or are guided exclusively by Christian values. Things have not changed that much since the time of Jesus.

It is noteworthy that the process of faith in Jesus continues to be a reality among Christians of today. There are some people who go to church on Sunday because they like the music or the rituals. Others go to church because it has become a place of meeting with friends or people of similar social background. Others go to church when a special need arises, such as an illness. Some go to church because otherwise they might be in mortal sin and go to hell; still others go to church attracted and moved by their love for Jesus whom they see as their only Lord and Savior. During his ministry, Jesus was followed by all kinds of people for very varied motives. Jesus did not reject anyone (except the Pharisees who wanted only to trap and destroy him). We must always hope and work so that those who go to church for somewhat human motives will mature in their faith until they will see Jesus exclusively as the Savior who loved them and sacrificed himself for them.

104. What special message is in the parable of the Good Shepherd (Jn 10:1–39)?

The parable of the Good Shepherd is an enigmatic discourse (Jn 10:6). It opens speaking of the sheep and the fold, with a terminology that seems to make allusion to the Temple, the place where the Jews gathered. From there, Jesus will take out his sheep and they will listen to him with their hearts, and placing their faith in him, they will follow him.

This first section ends with Jesus as the gate of the fold (Jn 10:7–10); in this new section, it repeats and explains the preceding section. Jesus is the final messenger from God to bring salvation to believers. Outside Jesus no salvation is possible.

At the beginning of the parable, the strangers present the problem; later the problem consists of the thieves and robbers (see Jn 10:5). The sheep flee from the strangers; in the second half of the parable, the mercenary flees when he sees danger approaching.

In the psalms, the Israel of Exodus is the flock that God has brought out from Egypt. God is the shepherd of his people (see Psalm 23). The prophets announced that God would send a shepherd who would be sacrificed (see Zech 13:7–9). Like other faithful shepherds, God himself will become the shepherd of his people (see Ezek 34).

Jesus is the Good Shepherd (see Jn 10:11–14). He is the model, ideal, and generous shepherd who sacrifices everything for his sheep. The opposite of the Good Shepherd is the mercenary, who does not own the sheep and does not have a personal relationship with them; he only cares for his salary. Jesus owns his sheep because the Father has given them to him (see Jn 10:12–13; 6:37, 44, 65; 17:6–7). The sheep belong to him; he cares for them, will never abandon them, and will risk and sacrifice his life for their well-being.

The Good Shepherd has other sheep for which he also sacrifices himself (see Jn 10:16–21). They are sheep that will come to form one flock in one fold, with only one shepherd, with Jesus after his sacrifice for them (see Jn 11:52). It is worth noting that verse 10:16 is like a parenthetical comment between two references to the sacrifice of Jesus. Saint John probably was thinking of believers coming from paganism who would form one community gathered around the Word of Jesus. There can be only one flock and one shepherd. The Letter to the Ephesians expresses this same idea of the reunion of Jews and Gentiles forming one community with Jesus (see Eph 2:11–22).

105. Why is the resurrection of Lazarus such an important miracle (Jn 11)?

The resurrection of Lazarus foretells the resurrection of Jesus and of Christians. At the end of the first century, it was a consoling fact that believers could expect that Jesus, who one day had awakened his friend from the sleep of death, would also awaken them from their own death to be with Jesus forever.

The victory of Jesus over death—in the case of Lazarus—announces the total victory of Jesus in his own resurrection (see Jn 1:1–44). Bethany, here and in the dinner that will follow (see Jn 12:1–8), looks forward to the burial and resurrection of the Lord.

It is surprising that the resurrection of Lazarus is not mentioned in the synoptic Gospels, although the two sisters of Lazarus, Martha and Mary, appear in Luke's Gospel (see 10:38–42). It is possible that the synoptic writers deliberately chose to narrate the miracles of Jesus that happened only in his ministry in Galilee. In the early church, the great biblical scholar Origen connected the resurrection of Lazarus with the parable of the rich man and Lazarus, found in Luke's Gospel (see 16:19–31); in that parable, the rich man asks Abraham that Lazarus be returned to life, to lead his brothers to conversion.

When Jesus heard the news of the sickness of his friend, he did not go to Bethany right away. He waited to arrive until Lazarus had been four days in his tomb; according to Jewish belief of the time, after three days, there was no hope that a person could come back to life.

It is worth noting how Jesus related to each of the two sisters, Martha and Mary. Jesus relates to each woman at her own level. With talkative Martha, Jesus speaks at length; with Mary, the woman of sensitive feelings, Jesus cries. Jesus does with them what Hispanics say when they attend a funeral: They go to accompany the family in their feelings.

Before the sepulcher of Lazarus, Jesus suffers "agony" in the fourth Gospel. Jesus was deeply moved and shaken before the tomb of his friend. The words of Saint John bring to mind the description of the agony of Jesus in the Garden of Gethsemani as narrated in the synoptic Gospels, when Jesus was shaken before his own death (see Mk 14:32–42). But before the sepulcher of Lazarus, it seems that the suffering of Jesus is not so much because of this dead friend but because of the spiritual death of those around him who were making comments showing their lack of faith (see Jn 11:36–39).

Another agony of Jesus in John's Gospel takes place on Palm Sunday after Jesus enters Jerusalem and goes to the Temple; some pagan "adorers" wanted to see him (see Jn 12:20–28). John seems to contrast the faith of the pagans who seek Jesus with the lack of faith of the Jews; this provokes an *agony* in Jesus. The last time Jesus is shaken and suffers what could be called an agony is during the Last Supper when he announces the betrayal of Judas (see Jn 13:21). Saint Luke, always close to the Gospel of John, says that Jesus cried and was deeply disturbed when he entered Jerusalem on Palm Sunday and saw the city from the Mount of Olives. Jesus cried because of the lack of faith of the city and the punishment that was coming (see Lk 19:41–44). The agonies of Jesus are not the fruit of his fears; they are caused by the lack of the people's faith and because of the future that is coming to them.

During the passion of Jesus, John's Gospel does not mention the agony in the Garden. The passion is the triumph and the glorification of Jesus that will culminate in Calvary.

106. What is the importance of the supper in Bethany, just before the passion of Jesus (Jn 12:1–8)?

Saint John tells the story of Jesus' supper at Bethany at the beginning of the last week of Jesus' life. It is based on traditional material that each evangelist narrates according to his theological aims. The anointing of Jesus by a woman is found in all four Gospels. Saint John connects it with the passion: it happens six days before the Passover of the death of Jesus, so that when Jesus enters Jerusalem, he is like an anointed king who goes to his sacrifice. The similarities and differences among the narratives of the evangelists are noteworthy:

MARK 14:3–8

While he was at Bethany in the house of Simon the leper, as he sat at the table, a woman came with an alabaster jar of very costly ointment of nard, and she broke open the jar and poured the ointment on his head. But some were there who said to one another in anger, "Why was the ointment wasted in this way? For this ointment could have been sold for more than three hundred denarii, and the money given to the poor." And they scolded her. But Jesus said, "Let her alone; why do you trouble her? She has performed a good service for me. For you always have the poor with you, and you can show kindness to them whenever you wish; but you will not always have me. She has done what she could; she has anointed my body beforehand for its burial."

JOHN 12:1–9

Six days before the Passover Jesus came to Bethany, the home of Lazarus, whom he had raised from the dead. There they gave a dinner for him. Martha served, and Lazarus was one of those at the table with him. Mary took a pound of costly perfume made of pure nard, anointed Jesus' feet, and wiped them with her hair. The house was filled with the fragrance of the perfume. But Judas Iscariot, one of his disciples (the one who was about to betray him), said, "Why was this perfume not sold for three hundred denarii and the money given to the poor?" (He said this not because he cared about the poor, but because he was a thief; he kept the common purse and used to steal what was put into it.) Jesus said, "Leave her alone. She bought it so that she might keep it for the day of my burial. You always have the poor with you, but you do not always have me."

LK 7:36–38

One of the Pharisees asked Jesus to eat with him, and he went into the Pharisee's house and took his place at the table. And a woman in the city, who was a sinner, having learned that he was eating in the Pharisee's house, brought an alabaster jar of ointment. She stood behind him at his feet, weeping, and began to bathe his feet with her tears and to dry them with her hair. Then she continued kissing his feet and anointing them with the ointment.

Saint John seems to indicate that the supper was not in the house of Lazarus, since Lazarus was an invited participant. Possibly, when Mary anointed Jesus, she was remembering the death of her own brother, while Jesus was thinking of his own death. Without realizing it, Mary was anointing Jesus in advance as king through his sacrifice and death. The royalty of Jesus is to be revealed in the passion (see Jn 18:33–37; 19:14–15, 19–22).

Saint John names Judas, pointing out that he was a thief in charge of the common purse of the group. At the Last Supper he will be named again as the treasurer of the group (thus in charge of the money). Judas had a good nose for business; when he smelled the perfume he knew its price. For him, money was the only thing that counted; love was an obstacle for business. For Mary, love was everything—money was secondary; this is why she squandered it to show her love for Jesus. Love and money are opposite poles in life. Jesus quoted Deuteronomy 15:11, pointing out that one who has true love for the poor will always find opportunities to practice that love.

107. Why did the Jews refuse to believe the message of Jesus (Jn 12:37–50)?

The lack of faith by the Jews was always a mystery for the first Christians. The Jews failed to believe and accept Jesus despite the many miracles they saw him perform. Saint Mark suggests an explanation of this fact through the Messianic secret: Jesus had performed miracles, but he forbade the people to publicize them. Saints Paul and Luke consider the incredulity of the Jews as something providential that served to open the door of the church to gentiles.

Saint John, especially at the end of the book of signs, proposes several explanations for the lack of faith of the Jews:

- They were not children of the light; they willingly remained in darkness.
- They refused conversion because their actions were evil.
- The Prophet Isaiah had already predicted it.
- Some Jews were cowards who did not come out openly to profess their faith. The fear of the Pharisees, the bitter enemies of Jesus, frightened them and made them keep their faith hidden.

- They preferred the glory of men to the glory of God.
- The Jews were part of the world that rejected Jesus.
- The Jews behaved like their ancestors in the Old Testament.

The central revelation by the evangelist is that Jesus is the light of the world (see Jn 8:12). This declaration is repeated to close the book of signs: "I have come as light into the world, so that everyone who believes in me should not remain in the darkness" (Jn 12:46).

108. Why does Saint John include the washing of the feet in his narrative of the Last Supper but does not speak of the Eucharist?

The Last Supper of Jesus is introduced with the announcement that the *hour* of Jesus has arrived (see Jn 13:1). It is the *hour*, the arrival of which was anticipated when Jesus entered Jerusalem on Palm Sunday (see Jn 12:23) and was acclaimed by the crowds as *King of Israel* (see Jn 12:13–15). The *hour* of Jesus is embraced at the Last Supper with the farewell discourse, the passion, and the resurrection. At the Last Supper Jesus is a presence that transcends the disciples (see Jn 16:4; 17:11). The risen and glorious Jesus also presents himself as one who has not yet gone up to the Father (see Jn 20:17). When the *hour* of Jesus arrives, Jesus is at the same time human and divine, present and absent.

From the beginning of the supper, as during the passion, Jesus is in total control of the events that transpire. The devil had his plans (see Jn 13:2), but he could not prevent the realization of the plan of Jesus and of his way of returning to the Father from whom he had come. Jesus gives the disciples a lesson in humility and service; the disciples do not understand him. Saint Peter seems to suspect that there was something mysterious in the action of Jesus, and after his first resistance, he submits completely to the will of Jesus. The love of Jesus in washing their feet was transparent. Later, Saint Peter says that he is ready to follow the Lord even in death, not realizing his own weakness and the intention of Jesus. In the future, it will not be a question of dying with or for Jesus but, as Jesus is going to do in his sacrifice, it will be a question of dying for his brothers.

Judas is presented from the beginning as one who carries out the plans of the devil. Later Judas will be declared possessed by the devil because Satan had entered into him (see Jn 13:27). Judas left the supper—it was night— and became part of the infernal darkness of that night.

Saint John does not tell of the institution of the Eucharist during the Last Supper as the other Gospels do. For Saint John, the washing of the feet symbolizes the communion of the disciples with Jesus, in sacrifice and service, which were associated with the Eucharist. John had already presented (in the sixth chapter) his interpretation of the Eucharist after the multiplication of the bread. In the synoptic Gospels, the breaking of the bread will continue to be done in memory of Jesus. In Saint John's Gospel, Jesus wants his disciples to continue washing the feet of each other, following his own example of humility and sacrifice.

109. Is there more than one discourse by Jesus in the dialogue that follows the Last Supper (Jn 13—17)?

"Rise, let us be on our way" (Jn 14:31). These words of Jesus in the midst of the dialogue or discourse of the Last Supper, in addition to the apparent contradictions and repetitions in the discourse (see Jn 13:36; 16:5, 4–24), have inclined some to think that the Gospel text includes a double discourse of Jesus that existed before the Gospel was written and which the evangelist incorporated into his work. But the discourse, as we have it now in John's Gospel, is strong connected and is composed of two clearly defined sections. The first part includes John 13:31—15:10 and the second consists of John 15:12—16:33. The center of the discourse in its present form is John 15:11, a text mentioned previously that repeats one of the basic ideas of the evangelist: "I have said these things to you so that my joy may be in you, and that your joy may be complete."

Both parts of the discourse begin by stressing the new commandment of fraternal love in imitation of the example of Jesus. Love and service will be distinctive characteristics of the disciples of Jesus.

The first part of the discourse explains how the disciples of Jesus will relate to him during his physical absence through a vision of faith (see Jn 14:9, 19). This physical absence is necessary for a new and greater spiritual presence through faith. The evangelist repeats the verb *remain* many times because in the same way as the Son remains, and is one in love with the Father, the disciples are going to live in communion and love with Jesus; through their communion with Jesus they will also be in communion with the Father (see Jn 14:6). The sacrifice of Jesus will be his return to the Father from whom he has come; this return will inaugurate the new mode of presence and communion.

The first part of the discourse tells how the Paraclete or Consoler (whom the Father will send to them) will enlighten them with regard to the past, so that they will come to the fullness of truth, reminding them of the message of Jesus: that Jesus lives, that they themselves will live, and will be in communion with Jesus and with the Father. This communion demands an assimilation of the words of Jesus (see Jn 15:7). Love will be the keystone for this new relationship and understanding; love will be the living witness of their life of faith (see Jn 13:34–35; 15:12–17).

In the second part of the discourse, communion with Jesus results in the disciples' charge to go out into the world to continue Jesus' mission and to bear witness of their faith in him. Mutual love will be the first form of witnessing to the world. The response of the world to the love of Christians will be one of hate and persecution; the world will treat the disciples in the same way Jesus had been treated. The suffering and death of the disciples, as in the case of Jesus, will be the gate toward a new life.

In the second section, the presence and action of the Paraclete, the Holy Spirit, which Jesus himself will send to them, will enable them to confront the world with its sins and injustices; they will conquer the world because the victory has been already achieved by Jesus.

110. What are the special dimensions of Jesus' new commandment of love at the Last Supper (Jn 15:12–17)?

In the dialogue with Nicodemus, Jesus had announced the love of God for the world when he gave his beloved son to save the world (see Jn 3:16). In the book of signs, Jesus speaks often of his love for the Father and of the love of the Father for his Son. At the Last Supper Jesus speaks often of the love that the disciples have received from the Father and from Jesus, a love they must share with each other. During supper Jesus tells the disciples how the love of the Father comes to the world; he explains what kind of love he has in mind while giving the new commandment of love. The love of the Father for the world passes through the love of Jesus: "As the Father has loved me, so I have loved you; abide in my love" (Jn 15:9). Jesus offers himself as the model of love: "This is my commandment, that you love one another as I have loved you" (Jn 15:12).

The love Jesus speaks about has four important characteristics:

1. It is a sacrificial love that gives his life for his own.
2. It is a love that includes obedience to Jesus, just as Jesus obeys the Father.
3. It is a revealing love that keeps no secrets; Jesus has made known to the disciples everything he has heard from the Father.
4. This love is a commitment, the fruit of an election and a decision; it will not be affected by the infidelity of the disciples a few hours later, during the passion.

These are the qualities that define true love in imitation of Jesus. Where there is no sacrifice, mutual obedience, openness without secrets, and fidelity at all costs, that type of love will have to be questioned.

111. Is the priestly prayer of Jesus his last will and testament (Jn 17:1–26)?

The prayer of Jesus at the end of the Last Supper has been called the testament of Jesus or his last will. It is also a model of prayer for Christians. The prayer follows the pattern of the discourse of the supper. The first part of the prayer refers to the physical absence of Jesus, while the theme of the second part is the mission of the disciples and the hatred of the world, because the disciples no longer belong to the world. The prayer has three sections, with an introduction and a conclusion:

- 17:1–3: Introduction
- 17:4–8: Jesus recalls his mission: give glory and reveal the Father.
- 17:9–19: Jesus prays for his disciples: Protect them and sanctify them.
- 17:20–23: Jesus prays for the believers of the future: that they may be one, that they may achieve perfect unity.
- 17:24–26: Conclusion

Jesus begins by giving thanks to the Father for his own fidelity to the mission entrusted to him. He also gives thanks for his disciples whom he sees as a gift from the Father, although he knows that three hours later they will abandon, betray, and deny him. The last section stresses Jesus' desire for unity among his disciples. When Saint John was writing his second edition of the Gospel, the first Christian sects, separated from the apostolic churches, had started to appear. For Saint John, anyone who had left the community was going against the desires and prayers of Jesus; Saint John calls the deserters from the community "antichrists." Faithful Christians were to have no contact with them (see 1 Jn 2:18–19; 2 Jn 7–11).

Like the discourse at the Last Supper, the priestly prayer opens with the themes of the absence of Jesus (see Jn 17:11). In the middle of the prayer, Jesus speaks of the joy of his disciples; this will be a distinctive characteristic, as important as love.

In the second part of the prayer, Jesus speaks of the hatred of the world for the disciples, who no longer belong to the world (see Jn 17:14). The prayer ends by reiterating the theme of love that had opened the narrative of the Last Supper (see Jn 13:1). The mutual presence of Jesus and the disciples is verified through love. The last desire of Jesus is to live in his own, and that his own will live in him. The mutual indwelling of Jesus with the disciples is patterned after Jesus' own indwelling with the Father. One way of understanding this mutual indwelling with Jesus could be considering what happens when a sponge is placed in a pail of water. Is the sponge in the water, or is the water in the sponge? Both!

112. What is the principal message of the narration of the passion in Saint John's Gospel (Jn 18:1-11)?

The introduction of the passion offers a theological perspective on the meaning of the sacrifice of Jesus. The elements mentioned by John at the opening of the passion have great significance.

The passion begins and ends with the mention of a garden (see Jn 18:1; 19:41). It seems the evangelist wants readers to think of that first garden where humanity disobeyed God and was defeated by the devil. Now Jesus, through his obedience to the Father, will conquer the devil and will redeem the fallen humanity.

Saint John calls attention to the darkness of that night, even if there might have been a full moon. The soldiers carry lanterns and torches (and arms), but these lights cannot overcome the darkness that covers everything. Saint Mark mentions the swords and the sticks. Judas is contrasted with Jesus; one is in front of the other (Jn 18:5). Judas, since the Last Supper, has become possessed by the devil, since when he ate the bread Jesus gave him, Satan entered into him (see Jn 13:27). The real struggle and confrontation in the passion is going to be between Jesus and the devil. When Jesus said "I AM," with words that had divine connotation, Jesus throws down Satan and his followers. The passion is the victory of Jesus over evil. It is also the salvation of his disciples, since this is the goal of his sacrifice (see Jn 18:8–9).

Saint John does not mention an agony in the garden. The only word John has in common with the synoptic narrative is the "chalice" that Jesus is going to drink. In John's Gospel, the chalice is almost a gift from the Father that Jesus accepts willingly. From the beginning, Jesus' enemies fall to the ground and they will be able to do only what Jesus will allow them.

113. How and when did Peter's denials of Jesus take place (Jn 18:15–27)?

When we compare the narrations of the four Gospels, it is not clear what happened on the night of Jesus' arrest. Was Jesus arrested and judged at midnight after his arrest, as Saints Matthew and Mark relate (see Mt 26:57–68; Mk 14:53–65)? Was Jesus judged early in the morning of the next day, as Saint Luke narrates it (see Lk 22:66–71)? Saint John, possibly with better knowledge of the people involved in the action against Jesus, says that Jesus was brought first to the high priest Annas; this man was at the time the most important leader of the priestly class in Jerusalem.

Saint John uses the denials of Peter as a framework for the declaration of Jesus before Annas the high priest. When Annas questions Jesus about his doctrine and his disciples, Jesus answers by appealing to the witness of those who have heard everything that he has taught in public. Peter should have been the best-informed person about Jesus' teachings, since he had been always with him. The tragedy, then and now, is that the disciple does not speak as he is expected to do, saying "I AM," like Jesus says so many times in the Gospel. Peter answers the priest "I am NOT" because by speaking like Jesus he would get into serious trouble. Since the passion and all throughout history, Jesus is not going to speak personally; he wants the testimony about him to be given by his disciples, by those who believe in him.

114. What was the process of Jesus before Pilate really like? (Jn 18:28—19:16)?

Jesus' trial before the Roman governor, Pilate, is narrated artistically by Saint John. The evangelist has composed seven scenes or mini-dialogues with Pilate, marked by the Greek word *elthen* ("went"), saying that Pilate went *in* and *out* of his palace to speak with the Jews, who had refused to go into the office of a pagan so that they would not become ritually impure. The evangelist presents the following order:

(1) *Outside* (Jn 18:28–32): Pilate, Jesus, and the Jews;
  an accusation that seeks the death of Jesus.
  (2) *Inside* (Jn 18:33–37): Pilate and Jesus: "Are you a king?"
  Jesus speaks saying that he is a king/teacher who has no subjects
  but disciples who listen to him.
    (3) *Outside* (Jn 18:38–40): Pilate and the Jews;
      the innocence of Jesus. Barabbas preferred to Jesus,
      a fighter for a kingdom of this world.
      (4) *(Inside)* (Jn 19:1–3): Jesus and the soldiers:
        Crowned and greeted as a king, with the royal insignia
        of the mantle and the crown.
      (5) *Outside* (Jn 19:4–7): Pilate, Jesus, and the Jews: The in-
      nocence of Jesus; he is the Son of Man and the Son of God.
      (6) *Inside* (Jn 19:8-11): Pilate and Jesus: "Where are you
      from?" Jesus speaks saying that all comes from above.
    Desire of Pilate to free Jesus.
    (7) *Outside* (Jn 19:12–16): Pilate, Jesus, and the Jews:
  The day, hour and place, of Pilate's proclamation of Jesus as King.
Jesus will go to his death for being a King.

Jesus is the king/teacher who reigns over the hearts of his disciples and not over the world. His reign comes when his own listen to his voice and they do his will (Our Father: *Thy Kingdom come, thy will be done*). The soldiers and Pilate pronounce great truths about Jesus without realizing the full meaning of their statements. The Jewish leaders, official Judaism, with an implicit blasphemy, since God was the only King of Israel, reject Jesus and accept Caesar as their king.

115. What special message is seen in John's narration of Jesus' crucifixion (Jn 19:18–37)?

The events on Calvary as related by Saint John seem to have as their goal an explanation of the kingdom of Jesus, announced in the trial before Pilate, and who are members of that kingdom. Saint John presents Calvary as a stage, with the cross of Jesus at its center. He narrates five incidents or scenes there in such a way that, in each incident, he presents a quality that distinguishes that kingdom. It is obvious that the first incident did not take place on Calvary but happened in the palace of the governor. Pilate did not go to Calvary. Saint John clarifies who are the citizens of Christ's kingdom, for Jesus reigns from a wood, as the old liturgy used to tell us:

1. *First scene* (Jn 19:18–22): Jesus is King—All languages and peoples must recognize him as such. Saint John has carefully arranged this event in a concentric narration with the mention of the languages at its center:

    (a) Pilate *wrote* a title and placed it on the cross
      (b) Jesus of Nazareth, *King of the Jews*....
        (c) Many *Jews* read it....
          (d) It was written in *Hebrew, Latin, and Greek*....
        (c') The high priests of the *Jews said to Pilate*
      (b') Do not write *King of the Jews*
    (a') What I have *written,* remains written.

    The kingdom of Jesus, as the whole world should understand, is UNIVERSAL.

2. *Second scene* (Jn 19:23–24): The robe of Jesus must not be torn or divided (in Jn 7:43 and in 9:16, the Jews are divided). In 1 Kgs 11:29–39, the division of a garment is a symbol for the division of Israel at the death of Solomon.

    The kingdom of Jesus will be characterized by UNITY. For Saint John, those who leave the community or break its unity no longer belong to the kingdom of Jesus.

138 · GETTING TO KNOW JESUS

3. *The third scene* (Jn 19:25–27): This dialogue between Jesus and his mother announces a new maternity for Mary. Jesus had come to form the last and eschatological family of God on earth. Christians are to have the same Father and the same Mother as Jesus; they are fully brothers and sisters of Jesus. The disciple received Mary as his mother. It will be the duty of all Christians to accept the mother of Jesus as their own mother. When the hour of Jesus comes, the role of Mary announced in Cana is fulfilled in Calvary. The hour of Jesus is the hour of the motherhood of Mary. As she did at Cana, she will continue to tell Christians to do what Jesus says, and she will tell Jesus the needs or lacks of Christians.

    The community over which Jesus reigns is a new spiritual FAMILY, in which the mother of Jesus has a most important role.

4. *Fourth scene* (Jn 19:28–30): Saint John speaks of the thirst of Jesus and the action of the soldiers; the scene culminates in the death of Jesus when "he gave up his Spirit." Jesus had said that if anyone was thirsty and came to him, he would receive the Spirit (Jn 7:37–39). In the midst of his thirst, Jesus gives the Spirit to his disciples. The community and family of Jesus is going to be guided by the Spirit, much more than by texts and laws who could lead to death.

    The community of Jesus will be guided by the inspiration of the Spirit of Jesus, by his SPIRITUALITY.

5. *Fifth scene* (Jn 19:31–37): Jesus did not have his legs broken. One of the soldiers pierced his side, and blood and water flowed from him. For Saint John, these two elements are sacramental and point toward the Eucharist and baptism (1 Jn 5:6–9).

    The community of Jesus enjoys SACRAMENTALITY.

    Summing up the evangelist's teaching, the events of Calvary tell us that the community of Jesus, the citizens of his kingdom, are people who come from every nation and language, who remain united, as the new family of Jesus, guided by his Spirit, and who celebrate the memory and presence of Jesus through certain sacraments.

116. How is the resurrection of Jesus described in John's Gospel (Jn 20:1–31)?

When narrating the resurrection of Jesus, Saint John tries to present, as if in slow motion, what really had happened on Calvary in the center of the hour of Jesus. On Calvary, Jesus died and began a new kind of life. Jesus went from this world to the Father without abandoning his own; Jesus gave his Spirit to Mary and the beloved disciple present there.

The Paschal Mystery of Jesus is centered in the cross. What Saint Luke narrates in a chronological order is presented theologically by Saint John. Saint Luke separates the death from the resurrection (three days); forty days later is the ascension, and ten days later is Pentecost. The Catholic Church celebrates this chronology of feasts in the annual liturgy. Saint John sees the entire mystery of Christ condensed in Calvary, as the Catholic Church celebrates it in every Mass, in the moment of consecration, as the Eucharistic prayer continues by saying: "*We celebrate the memory of Christ, your Son. We, your people and your ministers, recall his passion, his resurrection from the dead, and his ascension into glory....*"

Once again, Saint John offers five short narrations as a way to present the significance of the death and resurrection of Jesus:

1. The *empty tomb* (Jn 20:1–9) must lead the disciples to look for Jesus in a new manner. The beloved disciple "saw and believed" (Jn 20:8). In line with John's thoughts of theology, the risen Jesus is not to be found in the physical world: Jesus is in the heart of each believer; there, he can be found through an intimate contact of faith, just as Jesus had hinted at the end of his priestly prayer (Jn 17:26).

2. The *apparition of Jesus to Mary Magdalene* (Jn 20:10–18) presents a Jesus who is in this world and who has not yet gone up to the Father, but he is already on the way to him: "Do not hold on to me, because I have not yet ascended to the Father. But go to my brothers and say to them, 'I am ascending to my Father and your Father, to my God and your God'" (Jn 20:17). Mary Magdalene must bring this message to the other disciples. Here, Saint John, for the first time, tells us that the Father of Jesus is also our Father (Saint Matthew reveals that God is our Father at the beginning of his Gospel in the

Sermon on the Mount). After the events of Calvary, and the hour of Jesus, believers are all fully brothers and sisters of Jesus.

3. The *central apparition* (Jn 20:19–23) presents a glorious Jesus who is already with the Father. Jesus had said during the Last Supper that he would be sending them the Spirit after he went to the Father (Jn 16:7). In this apparition Jesus baptizes the disciples with the Holy Spirit, just as Jesus had been baptized in the Jordan River; he entrusts to them the mission of continuing his struggle against the world and sin. After Jesus' resurrection (after the event of Calvary), the disciples are the ones chosen by Jesus, as Jesus had been chosen by the Father. They will continue Jesus' mission of taking away the sins of the world. The resurrected Jesus is now incarnated and continues to work through his disciples.

4. The *apparition to Saint Thomas* (Jn 20:24–29) presents a glorious Jesus, Lord and God, always present though invisible to the physical eyes. Jesus knows everything Thomas has said to the other disciples when he thought Jesus was away. Thomas, like Mary Magdalene, had searched for the wrong Jesus. Mary Magdalene was looking for a corpse, while Thomas was looking for the same physical Jesus he had known before; he did not realize that, after the passion, Jesus had been transformed. Thomas' principal sin was that he had refused to believe the witness of his companions. The future of the Church depends on, and passes through, the witnessing of some and the faith of those who listen to the witness. There is a duty to give witness and to teach, but there is a corresponding duty of listening and of opening oneself to faith.

5. Saint John concludes his Gospel (Jn 20:30–31) by pointing out that, from now on, the testimony about Jesus, a channel for faith, is the Gospel he has written. Just as the empty tomb was an indication that Jesus had to be found elsewhere and in another form, the written Gospel leads readers to find Jesus in their lives of faith.

117. Is it true that chapter 21 of John's Gospel was added later?

Chapter 21 of John's Gospel, after the conclusion at the end of John 20:31, was added in the second and final edition of the Gospel to respond to the anxieties of the community after the death of the beloved disciple. The vocabulary of this chapter is noticeably different from the one used in the rest of the Gospel. The contents of this chapter are in contrast with some of the facts we know from the Gospel:

1. The new apparition of Jesus, we are told, is the third one after his resurrection. But Jesus had already appeared to Mary Magdalene, to the ten disciples, and to Thomas.
2. The disciples who had already seen Jesus twice in the Upper Room did not recognize him, even though they had received the Holy Spirit. However, the beloved disciple has an intuition about the identity of Jesus.
3. It is surprising that the disciples had already abandoned Jerusalem and had returned to their former activities and way of life.
4. The beloved disciple is already the determining factor in the unity and the faith of the community.

Answering the doubts and challenges of the community, the author of this chapter presents the theme of the mission of the disciples after the glorification of Jesus, the role of Peter in the community after his triple denial, and the role of the beloved disciple in the birth and strengthening of the community.

The miraculous catch of fish is parallel to the vocation and mission of the disciples in the first miracle of Jesus in the Gospel of Luke (see Lk 5:1–11). In John's Gospel, this miraculous catch announces the universal mission and unity of the Church that gathers in Jesus. The universality is probably signified in the 153 fish caught. This number happens to be the sum of the first seventeen numbers (1–17), a number very appropriate to allude to the fullness and universality of the mission. The net that was not torn points to the unity of the community.

Saint Peter needed to be rehabilitated after his denials of Jesus in the passion. The failure of the apostle is remedied by his triple confession of love. By the time this chapter was added to the Gospel, Saint Peter had followed Jesus by dying on a cross.

The beloved disciple died shortly before this chapter was added. The author wants to explain that his death was not something unexpected; some had misunderstood the words of Jesus and thought that the disciple would be alive until the second coming of Jesus.

118. How can we know better the Jesus of the Gospels?

The Gospel of Saint John teaches that a person may come to know Jesus in two ways: (1) living with Jesus and being united to him, and (2) doing what Jesus says, making his teachings part of one's daily life.

To live with Jesus, and to learn what Jesus says and teaches, we must know, almost by heart, all that the Gospels tell us about Jesus. As Saint Jerome reminded us, ignorance of the Gospels is ignorance of Christ.

The imitation of Jesus—doing what he did, speaking as he spoke, thinking as he thought, having the mind of Jesus—helps us to identify ourselves with him and his mission. A Christian is called to continue the incarnation of Christ in his or her own person.

Life in the community of believers, an active participation in the life of a Christian community, especially in the celebration of the sacraments, is a school of evangelization in which we are all disciples and in which Jesus teaches us through our own brothers and sisters.

A life of prayer and meditation, openness to the Holy Spirit who leads us to understand the fullness of Gospel truth revealed by Jesus, should lead us to fall in love with Jesus in the way he wants us to love him.

Finally, distancing ourselves from the materialism that surrounds us, a commitment to the causes of the poor and of simple people who place all their hope in the Lord will help us to know the Lord better. Jesus identified himself with the poor; for this reason, a commitment to the poor and their causes will help us to see more clearly the presence of Jesus in our surroundings, because Jesus, according to his desire and promise, continues alive with us and in us.